More Praise for

The Little Book
of Bull Moves in Bear Markets

"I don't always agree with Peter, but I always listen to what he has to say. Anyone who has a track record as good as his in predicting future pricing of commodities and equity markets cannot be ignored. We always look for ways to stay ahead of the market. This little book, written by someone whose prognostications have proven prescient, should be a part of formulating your strategy for the future."

David Asman, Fox Business and
Fox News anchor and host, and former
op-ed editor of the *Wall Street Journal*

"One of Wall Street's great straight shooters, Peter Schiff is a reliable source of unvarnished economic reality who has the common sense to yell "fire" when everyone else quibbles over the definition of "smoke.""

Paul Tharp, Financial Writer,
the *New York Post*

THE LITTLE BOOK
OF
BULL MOVES IN
BEAR MARKETS

Little Book Big Profits Series

In the *Little Book Big Profits* series, the brightest icons in the financial world write on topics that range from tried-and-true investment strategies to tomorrow's new trends. Each book offers a unique perspective on investing, allowing the reader to pick and choose from the very best in investment advice today.

Books in the *Little Book Big Profits* series include:

The Little Book That Beats the Market, where Joel Greenblatt, founder and managing partner at Gotham Capital, reveals a "magic formula" that is easy to use and makes buying good companies at bargain prices automatic, enabling you to successfully beat the market and professional managers by a wide margin.

The Little Book of Value Investing, where Christopher Browne, managing director of Tweedy, Browne Company, LLC, the oldest value investing firm on Wall Street, simply and succinctly explains how value investing, one of the most effective investment strategies ever created, works, and shows you how it can be applied globally.

The Little Book of Common Sense Investing, where Vanguard Group Founder John C. Bogle shares his own time-tested philosophies, lessons, and personal anecdotes to explain why outperforming the market is an investor illusion, and how the simplest of investment strategies can deliver the greatest return to the greatest number of investors.

The Little Book That Makes You Rich, where Louis Navellier, financial analyst and editor of investment newsletters since 1980, offers readers a fundamental understanding of how to get rich using the best in growth investing strategies. Filled with in-depth insights and practical advice, *The Little Book That Makes You Rich* outlines an effective approach to building true wealth in today's markets.

The Little Book That Builds Wealth, where Pat Dorsey, director of stock analysis for leading independent investment research provider Morningstar, Inc., guides the reader in understanding "economic moats," learning how to measure them against one another, and selecting the best companies for the very best returns.

The Little Book That Saves Your Assets, where David Darst, a managing director of Morgan Stanley who chairs the firm's Global Wealth Management Asset Allocation and Investment Policy Committee, explains the role of asset allocation in maximizing investment returns to meet life objectives. Brimming with the wisdom gained from years of practical experience, this book is a vital road map to a secure financial future.

The Little Book of Bull Moves in Bear Markets, where Peter D. Schiff, President of Euro Pacific Capital, Inc., looks at historical downturns in the financial markets to analyze what investment strategies succeeded and shows how to implement various bull moves so that readers can preserve, and even enhance, their wealth within a prosperous or an ailing economy.

THE LITTLE BOOK

OF
BULL MOVES IN
BEAR MARKETS

How to Keep Your Portfolio Up

When the Market Is Down

PETER D. SCHIFF

A Lynn Sonberg Book

WILEY

John Wiley & Sons, Inc.

Copyright © 2008 by Peter D. Schiff and Lynn Sonberg Book Associates. All rights reserved.

Published by John Wiley & Sons, Inc., Hoboken, New Jersey.
Published simultaneously in Canada.

For general information on our other products and services or for technical support, please contact our Customer Care Department within the United States at (800) 762-2974, outside the United States at (317) 572-3993 or fax (317) 572-4002.

Wiley also publishes its books in a variety of electronic formats. Some content that appears in print may not be available in electronic books. For more information about Wiley products, visit our web site at www.wiley.com.

Library of Congress Cataloging-in-Publication Data:

Schiff, Peter D., 1963-
  The little book of bull moves in bear markets : how to keep your portfolio up when the market is down/Peter D. Schiff.
      p.   cm.—(Little book big profits series)
    ISBN 978-0-470-38378-0 (cloth)
    1. Investments. 2. Bear markets. I. Title.
  HG4521.S35134 2009
  332.6—dc22

                                                                        2008032169

Printed in the United States of America

10 9 8 7 6 5 4 3 2 1

To my brother Andrew Schiff, whose help has been instrumental in getting my message out, more recently as a valuable member of the Euro Pacific team, and to our parents, Irwin and Ellen Schiff, who, though divorced early on in our lives, nevertheless managed to maintain a sense of family that ultimately allowed this business relationship to flourish. I also want to especially thank my father, for his knowledge and passion, and for the personal sacrifice that he has made for his country. I hope that his grandchildren, including my son Spencer, my niece Eliza, and my nephew Ethan, will one day benefit from his courage.

Disclosure

─────────── ≈ ───────────

Data from various sources was used in the preparation of this book. The information is believed to be reliable, accurate, and appropriate, but it is not guaranteed in any way. The forecasts and strategies contained herein are statements of opinion, and therefore may prove to be inaccurate. They are in fact the author's own opinions, and payment was not received in any form that influenced his opinions. Peter Schiff and the employees of Euro Pacific Capital implement many of the strategies described. This book contains the names of some companies used as examples of the strategies described, as well as a mutual fund that can be sold only by prospectus; but none can be deemed recommendations to the book's readers. These strategies will be inappropriate for some investors, and we urge you to speak with a financial professional and carefully review any pertinent disclosures before implementing any investment strategy.

In addition to being the president, Peter Schiff is also a registered representative and owner of Euro Pacific Capital, Inc. Euro Pacific is a National Association of Securities Dealers (NASD)–registered broker-dealer and a member of the Securities Investor Protection Corporation (SIPC). This book has been prepared solely for informational purposes, and it is not an offer to buy or sell, or a solicitation to buy or sell, any security or instrument, or to participate in any particular trading strategy. Investment strategies described in this book may ultimately lose value even if the opinions and forecasts presented prove to be accurate. All investments involve varying amounts of risk, and their values will fluctuate. Investments may increase or decrease in value, and investors may lose money.

Contents

Foreword

❧

ONCE IN A GREAT while, the world undergoes big changes. The great discovery voyages at the end of the fifteenth century led to a huge enlargement of the world's economic sphere. Venice—master of the previously important Mediterranean trade routes, and the world's richest and most powerful city—was thrown into a corner of the world, as Voltaire later observed.

The breakdown of the socialist/communist ideology at the end of the twentieth century and the end of policies of self-reliance and isolation on the Indian subcontinent were other big changes. Suddenly, three billion ambitious and motivated people joined the world's free market economy and the capitalistic system. These new citizens of the global economy are striving mightily to raise themselves to the level of affluence they see in their Western counterparts. Simply put, the free world has been joined by more than three billion people who have a similar frame of mind as the American pioneers of the nineteenth century.

At the same time, as Peter Schiff so vividly shows in this book, economic policy makers in the United States have totally lost their way. No wonder that in recent years a new economic and financial anxiety has taken hold among those public citizens who try to understand the world around them. This confusion is largely a function of the increasingly incomprehensible explanations offered by the most powerful figures in government, academia, and commerce. Anyone who has recently listened to the 2008 speeches of Ben Bernanke, the chairman of the Federal Reserve Board, is familiar with the feeling. The large words flow, but the concepts never coalesce into anything that is meaningful even to those, like myself, who have studied economics.

As a result, many regular folks may be tempted to look at economics much as they look at quantum physics: concepts that lie beyond the reach of casual understanding. When the policies of the Federal Reserve seem to be counterintuitive, who can blame them? As an example, currently the Fed is obsessed with solving economic and financial problems with artificially low interest rates at a time when, because of the entry into the global economy of the three billion people I referred to earlier, inflationary pressures, especially on raw materials, are very high.

In fact, it would appear that academia has found a gold mine in transforming basic economics and the art of investment based on common sense into a science of finance, filling entire libraries with pages and pages of indecipherable equations. Government leaders have seized upon these theories as a means to deploy a smoke screen between their own actions and the impact those moves make on the economy.

However, we are fortunate to have someone like Peter Schiff, who shows us, with common sense and in a highly readable and focused account of economic and financial trends over the past few years, not only how to avoid costly investment mistakes, but how to capitalize on opportunities that will preserve and enhance our wealth.

Whereas many experts view the greed and irresponsibility of subprime lenders as the underlying cause of the current credit market turmoil, Peter vividly shows how the Fed, through irresponsible monetary policies, not only caused the credit crisis, but also destroyed the value of the dollar and fueled the staggering price increases in food and energy.

Why is this book so good? Because Peter Schiff has common sense and does not mince his words. With admirable clarity, sarcasm, and hard-hitting criticism of the Fed and other policy makers, he explains the causes and consequences of the current financial crisis and how you can find ways to preserve your capital. Schiff clearly understands that a big change in the world's economic and political equilibrium is under way and that such a change requires unconventional thinking and new investment strategies.

My advice is this: Listen to another incomprehensible speech by the chairman of Federal Reserve Board, and then read this book written by a businessman with common sense! You will then know why the U.S. economy is in so much trouble, what caused the financial crisis, and how you can prepare for the future. You will also lose all respect for the financial leaders in Washington and Wall Street who claimed wisdom but delivered only folly. Peter Schiff has written a true masterpiece.

—MARC FABER
Editor of the Gloom Boom & Doom Report

Author's Note

~

What Do We Mean by Bull and Bear Markets?

The Little Book of Bull Moves in Bear Markets is a book for stock investors; its focus is on preserving and enhancing invested wealth at a time when a collapsing American economy threatens to destroy it. The current economic backdrop requires a fresh approach to investing, and before getting too deeply into the discussion, I want to say a word about what I mean by the terms *bull* and *bear markets*.

Except in hindsight, nobody knows when bull, bear, or sideways markets begin and end, and there is no universal agreement on the magnitude or duration of the market moves that define them. But precise definitions are not terribly important as long as you know *bull* means up, *bear* means down, and *sideways* means flat, and you have the relative knowledge to distinguish market trends from reverse market movements and fluctuations that are merely short-term in nature.

Unless otherwise specified, *bull*, *bear*, and *sideways* refer in this book to the stock market, but the terms are commonly applied to markets in other asset classes and in stock market sectors, such as commodities; subsectors, such as gold; or stock classifications, such as small capitalization and large capitalization. Price movements are tracked by indexes and averages that measure changes using various weighting methodologies.

It is important, particularly when making period-to-period comparisons, to be consistent in the use of indexes. A broad market comparison using the price-weighted, high-capitalization Dow Jones Industrial Average of 30 stocks versus the capitalization-weighted Dow Jones Wilshire Index of 5000 equities would produce significant discrepancies, for example, even though the former is the world's most popular indicator of the market and the latter is the only index that includes all stocks traded in the market.

Broadly speaking, we have *secular bull or bear trends*, which are long-term and can last five to 20 years or more; *primary bull or bear trends*, which last from a few months to five years; and *secondary trends*, which are reverse movements of at least 10 percent, are measured in days or weeks, and are called *corrections* when they reverse a bull trend and *bear market rallies* when they reverse a bear trend.

Short-term fluctuations having no consistency in terms of direction come under the rubric of volatility. For example, a temporary drop in price, called a dip, has no forecasting value whatsoever, although it might be an opportunity to add to a position.

For price changes to be meaningful, nominal values must be converted to real numbers, meaning there has to be an adjustment for inflation. As discussed at length elsewhere in the book, when inflation lifts asset prices, this effect is not included in the consumer or producer price indexes used by government to measure it, so we have to estimate a realistic rate of actual inflation. Currently I estimate real inflation at between 8 and 10 percent despite the CPI reflecting only a mere fraction of that number, around 4 percent.

The importance of all these distinctions is that investors, unlike short-term traders, use strategies that attempt to synchronize holding periods with bull trends and stand to lose money if they seriously misjudge when the trends begin and end. A long-term investor playing a secular bull market, for example, must have enough confidence in the secular trend to recognize primary and secondary reversals for what they are and hang in there for the longer term. More germane to the current situation, long-term investors must understand the nature of the secular bear market now well under way, and resist the temptation to buy into the various upside reversals that occur along the way.

Because there is no way to identify the beginning or end of a trend except by a rearview mirror, making what are essentially market timing judgments requires courage and conviction in addition to understanding the underlying economic conditions and learning what we can from historical experience.

Wall Street is eager to save us such trouble, but is an unlikely source of reliable guidance. Like Merrill Lynch, Wall Street generally is "bullish on America." It wants its public to think we're either in a bull market or near the end of bear market, a happy choice between upward momentum and bargain prices, which is to say a market perennially favorable for buyers of what the Wall Street firms are selling. It's easy to sit here and dismiss their market wisdom as self-serving propaganda, but they are a relentless and persuasive source of plausible optimism, and it takes a lot of fortitude to resist being influenced by them.

The strategies I recommend in the pages that follow are based on my conviction that the U.S. dollar will continue to lose purchasing power as expansionist monetary policy, in a futile effort to revive our consumer-based economy, creates additional inflation. With the dollar on a clear path toward collapse, cash and bonds are held at one's peril; and the stock market, nominally in a bear market as of July 2, 2008, but off a whopping 42 percent from its January 14, 2000, high when adjusted for 8 percent annual inflation, has by my analysis been in a secular bear market since that date that that will last well into the next decade. Running concurrently, and spurred by the tremendous demand expected from industrial revolutions in China and India, has been a worldwide secular bull market in agricultural, natural resource, and precious metals commodities. My strategies aim to tap into that big-time by owning producing companies or stocks of conservative, dividend-paying utility or commercial real estate companies that benefit by being vital to the economies of resource-rich countries.

So throughout the book, when I talk about bull and bear markets in gold, oil, and various other commodities, I'll often use the terms loosely, referring to commodity prices as well as the share prices of companies producing those commodities. Unless otherwise specified, though, I'll be referring to markets secular in duration.

Some Historical Perspective

The worst bear market in history began with the Crash of 1929, which kicked off the Great Depression and ended when World War II began in the early 1940s, but

wartime rally was actually the primary trend within a secular bear market that lasted until 1949.

It is instructive to focus on the market's movements
in the 1930s as tracked by the Dow Jones Industrial Average. After peaking at 380 in 1929 following an eight-year
bull market, the Dow plunged by 90 percent to 42 late in
1932. But then it rallied to 187 in 1937, dropped to
around 100 a year later, had a couple of minor rallies,
and then bottomed at 95 in 1942. Extending the secular
bear market, another bear market rally took it to 206 by
1946, after which it pulled back to 167 and went sideways
until 1949, when it phased into a secular bull market last-
ing from 1950 to 1965.

That two major rallies occurred during the worst bear
market on record illustrates the importance of and diffi-
culty of recognizing trends for what, with the benefit of
hindsight, they turn out to be.

Another secular bear market extended from 1966,
when the Vietnam War was getting hot, to 1982, after
the Reagan-Volcker assault on double-digit inflation. Those
who think the cure was worse than the disease might take
another look at the disease. In nominal terms, the Dow
lost around 22 percent during the 16-year period. But the
CPI, a somewhat more reliable indicator of inflation then
than now, rose during the same period from 95.4 to 308.6,
a gain of 223.5 percent or 7.3 percent annualized, which

seems staggering and is, but is less than the real inflation rate prevailing today.

Four bear market rallies (which at the time fit the definitions of bull markets) occurred during the period, in 1967–1968, 1970–1973, 1974–1976, and, on a smaller scale, in 1980. In inflation-adjusted terms, however, the highs were lower than previous bull market peaks and the subsequent lows, including the infamous 1973–1974 bear market, were lower in real terms than previous bottoms.

Including a secular bear market from 1906 to 1921, there were three secular bear markets in the 100 years prior to the present one, and to be invested through any of them, especially when inflation is factored in, was very costly. To put this in perspective, and to show the dangers of overpaying for stocks at bull market peaks, the Dow was worth 20 ounces of gold in both 1929 and 1980, but bottomed at near one ounce of gold in 1932 and 1980. The recent bear market began with the Dow priced near 43 ounces of gold, and is worth less than 12 ounces today, on its way to retest the 1932 and 1980 lows. In other words, the Dow, despite a nominal rise from 380 in 1929 to about 11,000 today, has actually lost almost half its real value when measured from its peak price of 80 years ago. So much for the idea that buying stocks at any price always works provided your time horizon is long enough.

Conversely, we were in a secular bull markets between 1982 and 2000, in which stocks followed a ratchet pattern steeply upward. That period included the infamous Black Monday of October 19, 1987, when the Dow plunged 508 points or 22.6 percent, beginning a three-month correction reflecting worry about inflated stock prices, federal budget and trade deficits, and foreign market activity. The point drop set a record that was broken on Bloody Monday in 1997, when economic and currency upheaval in Southeast Asia triggered a 554-point drop. On a percentage basis, however, the 1987 drop was greater.

In 1990, after years of land speculation and other overinvestment had resulted in a bubble economy and subsequent liquidity crisis, the Tokyo stock market fell 36 percent, wiping out the yen equivalent of $2.07 trillion in value and marking the beginning or a severe recession and secular bear market lasting until 2000, when signs of recovery began to appear. Japan tried a number of stimulative measures, including lower interest rates, public works projects, structural reform policies, and other ideas, all of which contributed to huge government deficits, but its economy was very slow to respond, possibly because of a high savings rate, one respect in which Japan's experience and America's are dissimilar. Those Japanese investors who ignored the secular trend remained invested and suffered over a decade of losses. However, those who read the economic tea leaves sold their shares and used the proceeds to invest in bull markets elsewhere. That is precisely the course of action this book will encourage you to follow in our bear market.

As noted earlier, the U.S. stock market is eight years into a secular bear market, taking inflation into account, the economic background of which is covered in the following pages. The book focuses on strategies of mine that will help readers avoid getting hurt by the collapsing dollar and enable them to participate in bull markets elsewhere. The goal is to help you preserve and enhance wealth that can be reinvested in America after fundamental economic reform takes place.

Introduction

~

IF YOU LISTEN closely you can almost hear the hissing of a bubble deflating. But I'm not referring to either the housing or credit bubbles, though those are certainly losing air violently. My eyes are focused on a far bigger bubble, one that comprises the entire U.S. economy.

The problem with financial bubbles is that they can be very difficult to detect, especially for those trapped inside. The feeling of permanence can be so tangible and the new-era psychology so alluring that even the normally pragmatic get swept away. Even as the air seeps out, they rarely notice the contraction until it's too late. By then they are soaking wet, and once they wipe the soap from their eyes, they finally see the light. However, clarity of vision in retrospect does little good for investors who had placed their faith in a bubble that was in fact a false paradigm.

The current economic slowdown is being dismissed as the sort of cyclical decline that the American economy has shrugged off numerous times over the past generation and a half. Unfortunately, we will not be so fortunate this time around. It is in fact the beginning of the economic collapse that I foretold early last year in my first book, *Crash Proof: How to Profit from the Coming Economic Collapse* (John Wiley & Sons, 2007). Although many of the book's predictions were considered paranoid at the time, the collapse I envisioned is now well under way. The pace of change is slower than I imagined, but the script is playing out pretty much along the lines that I described it.

If you have not already read *Crash Proof*, I suggest that it would be an invaluable preparation to what I will discuss in the pages that follow. Because it was written before legions of failed mortgage lenders cashed their final checks, oil blew passed $100 per barrel heading for regions unknown, and the Federal Reserve stepped in to prevent complete seizure in the financial markets, reading it will give you a better understanding of the concepts discussed in this book and a greater appreciation for the clarity of my vision.

Most in my profession refrain from writing books that make bold economic or market predictions. The desire for literary fame and mantelpiece glory is overcome by the fear of leaving a written record of inaccurate forecasts. So read *Crash Proof* now, with the benefit of the hindsight I lacked when I wrote it, and you will appreciate this book all the more.

As the economic unease of 2008 takes hold across the country, mainstream media commentators, government officials, and my fellow Wall Street prognosticators are confident that government stimuli and accommodative Fed policy will revive the economy. After pushing these appropriate buttons, it is confidently assumed that consumers will once again spend freely, reviving the economy and the stock and real estate markets in the process. Here they confuse the symptom with the cure. As strange as it may sound in our postindustrial, credit-fueled, savings-depleted, shop-till-you-drop society, consumer spending in and of itself does not constitute an economy. Rather than being part of the solution, consumer spending is a major contributor to our current malaise.

In *Crash Proof* I referred to our nation as America. com and compared our economy to a house of cards, impressive on the outside, but a disaster waiting to happen beneath the surface. Those descriptions were apt in that our entire economy was built on a phony foundation of

debt-financed consumption. While most economists mar-
veled at how much money Americans were spending, I
was shocked by how much we were borrowing. While others extolled the value of our assets (stock prices and home
equity), I recognized those asset values as fleeting and
instead was horrified by liabilities that we were incurring.
While stock prices could fall and home equity vanish, the
liabilities associated with those assets would remain. In
fact, given the short-term nature of the debts, and the negative amortization features of many mortgages, liabilities
and the cost of serving them would actually grow even as
the values of the assets securing them shrank.

The basic problem was that almost everyone confused
reckless consumption with legitimate economic growth,
and asset bubbles with genuine wealth creation. Flush
with home equity and emboldened by rock-bottom teaser
rates, American homeowners acted as if they had won the
lottery. They made rash decisions and spent lavishly,
based on ridiculous assumptions that they are only now
beginning to comprehend.

The phantom wealth created by booming real estate
values engendered massive spending on nonproductive
consumer goods, such as residential real estate, home remod-
eling, appliances, plasma TVs, SUVs, vacations, clothing, food, and energy. However, now that home equity is
disappearing and teaser rates are resetting, we simply

cannot afford to pay the money back—and even if we could, doing so would be a drag on our economy for years to come. More importantly, our creditors are arriving at the same conclusion and cutting off the funding.

As this recession gathers momentum, the American economy will be seen as the paper tiger that it is. The myth of the heroic American consumer, carrying the rest of the world along in the bed of his half-ton pick up truck, will finally be shattered. Rather then being the source of our prosperity, he will be appreciated as having been a driving force in its destruction. Those who made stock and real estate investments based on faith in his resilience will lose their money along with their naiveté. Those who directly underwrote his profligacy based on sophisticated computer models will lose even more. Lenders will rediscover the prudence of prior generations, as it becomes painfully clear that banking is not really about lending money at all, but about getting paid back.

Of course consumers did not act alone but were empowered, in fact cheered on by our own government, the Federal Reserve in particular. By keeping interest rates artificially low, borrowers were rewarded and savers were punished. Speculators got rich while savers were left wanting.

The greater problem, of course, is that few in power actually understand how we got into this mess, and those few may lack the courage to speak up. As a result, the next several years will be increasingly difficult as the various proposed government cures will only worsen the underlying economic disease and delay any meaningful recovery.

Therefore, do not expect that the American economy will stumble upon a reservoir of unnoticed credit, and that we will once again spend away the pain. Do not follow the typical Wall Street buy-and-hold mantra and the advice to simply ride out the economic storm. This is a category five monster, and it will destroy all who foolishly remain in its path. This is not the time to hunker down, but to simply get out of the way and let the storm pass you by. This book will show you not only where to go, but how to get there.

Chapter One

Let's Do the Time Warp Again

～

What Happened to Our Purchasing Power?

THE *NEW YORK TIMES* "Week in Review" section over Memorial Day weekend 2008 reprinted a cartoon from the *Atlanta Journal-Constitution* showing a single-family house roped to the roof of an SUV. In the image, the hapless driver explains to a puzzled passerby, "I couldn't afford a fill-up so I bought a house instead."

It's comical because of its incongruity, but the realities that inspired it are anything but laughable. I'd call it gallows humor, and the dark side is dark indeed.

Unless I'm terribly wrong—and my predictions have been uncannily accurate in the past—skyrocketing gasoline and food prices and plummeting home sales are among the early symptoms of fundamental economic problems that are too advanced to be reversible and grave enough to profoundly impact the living standards of most Americans for years to come.

In the chapters that follow, my focus will be on where to put your money at a time when the American economy is flat broke and the wealth creation is happening elsewhere. To appreciate the urgency and cogency of my advice, however, you've got to understand what went wrong and how much worse it's going to get. That's what this chapter is about.

In my book *Crash Proof: How to Profit from the Coming Economic Collapse* (John Wiley & Sons, 2007), which was published when all seemed quiet on the economic front, I set forth in detail my contrary position that "The economy of the United States, long the world's dominant creditor, now the world's largest debtor, is fighting a losing battle against trade and financial imbalances that are growing daily and are caused by dislocations too fundamental to reverse."

Observing that the bulk of the deterioration had occurred, almost unnoticed, in the short space of two decades, a period that most Americans experienced as prosperity, I compared the 2006 economy to a giant bubble in search of a pin. Real estate prices had risen to absurd levels, driven by a reckless Federal Reserve, artificially low mortgage rates, lax and sometimes fraudulent lending practices, and massive speculation. Trade and budget deficits were huge, persistent, and growing; and the national debt, payable in large part to our trading partners, had reached dangerous levels. Aggressive monetary policy was initially showing up in rising asset prices not reflected in the consumer price index (CPI). Consumer debt was fueling consumer spending that the government was misrepresenting as legitimate economic growth signifying a healthy economy. The dollar was already losing altitude and poised to head into a tailspin.

In general, the American economy was on a course toward either stagflation—a combination of recession and inflation reminiscent of the 1970s—or, worse, hyper-inflation, similar to what happened to Argentina early in this decade, when a middle class literally went to bed well-fed and happy and then woke up threatened with poverty.

The Healthy 1950s

To understand the why and how of what happened to the American economy, take a look back at a time when it was rosy with good health, the postwar 1950s.

With pent-up demand from wartime shortages and with everybody having babies, consumer spending was strong, manufacturing was thriving, and economic growth was at an all-time high. The savings rate was positive, providing investment capital for new industries like aviation and electronics. Unemployment was well in check. Blue collar wages and white collar incomes were rising, and the housing industry was booming. Inflation was low (an obsession of President Eisenhower) and fiscal discipline kept interest rates moderate. The stock market gained. The national debt was negligible. The federal budget was tightly controlled and generally in balance. Much more was exported than imported, and the balance of trade had large surpluses. (A note to economic purists: The *current account,* which term is frequently used synonymously with the *trade account,* was running deficits. That was because the current account comprises, in addition to the trade account, the *financial account.* In the 1950s, the financial account reflected the Marshall Plan and other recovery-related foreign aid, foreign direct investment, and military investment abroad. The current account deficit was not deleterious to the country's economic health.)

The dollar, the world's reserve currency following the Bretton Woods agreements in 1944, was backed by gold and in strong demand, and the United States Treasury held better than 60 percent of the world's foreign currency reserves.

So the 1950s economy was robust, but still there were harbingers of challenges to come. The first credit card, for example, was issued in 1950 and by the end of the decade, consumer credit had become an important part of the economy. Although manufacturing production was the dominant factor in economic growth, the service sector, which paid lower wages and produced little that was exportable, was gaining importance as the number of service employees surpassed the number producing goods by mid-decade. Massive government spending for highways, airports, and social welfare programs was causing huge tax increases.

The Coming Economic Collapse

Fast-forward now to early 2007 when my book *Crash Proof: The Coming Economic Collapse*, was published.

By then, the nation had undergone a radical transformation in terms of its economic infrastructure and its economic behavior. A service-based economy had largely supplanted one based on manufacturing that was now at a competitive disadvantage to producers in Asia and elsewhere who were less burdened by regulation, high taxes, and mandated worker benefits. America had become a nation of consumers, and producers were disappearing.

To say the United States government was operating on borrowed money and dangerously dependent on foreign suppliers and lenders was to make the understatement of the new millennium.

Reflecting that reality the balance of trade was running huge deficits, with imports exceeding exports by some $800 billion annually. Federal budget deficits ranged between $300 billion and $400 billion yearly, caused by trillions of dollars of government spending for the Iraq and Afghanistan wars, entitlement programs, debt service, and other expenses. The national debt, owed in large part to China and other trading partners, exceeded $9 trillion, a staggering and unrepayable figure yet only a small part of the overall debt picture. Unfunded liabilities, such as Social Security, veteran benefits, and loan guarantees, raised total government obligations to over $50 trillion. Foreign currency reserves held by the United States Treasury declined to a mere 1 percent of world reserves, ranking the United States behind Libya, Poland, and Turkey.

The stock market, following the longest bull market in history, was still overvalued, even though a bubble in the (mainly) NASDAQ-listed dot-com issues had finally burst in 2000. This caused a short-lived technical recession, which the Federal Reserve quickly replaced with an even larger bubble, this one in residential real estate.

So to say the United States government was operating on borrowed money and dangerously dependent on foreign suppliers and lenders was to make the understatement of the new millennium. On a personal level, the American population was up to its eyeballs in debt and the national savings rate had just turned negative for the first time ever. The real estate bubble, the biggest speculative mania in United States history, had just burst, though few seemed to notice. The dollar was in a steep decline and on a path to collapse, but the economy was too vulnerable to risk raising rates.

Still, the government economic leaders said not to worry. Consumer spending was strong, and increases in the gross domestic product (GDP) reflected healthy economic growth, they said. Moreover, we were told, household net worth was at an all-time high, reflecting the strength of the real estate market and steady growth of home equity.

Doctor Doom

With a new book to plug, I was appearing more than ever on CNBC and other TV venues, where I gave bearish symmetry to panels of experts who were almost invariably bullish. CNBC dubbed me "Doctor Doom."

To peals of the old horse laugh, I argued until I was blue in the face that all the happy talk was an ominous misreading of the realities. As fellow panelists cited GDP growth as evidence of a strong economy, I countered that 70 percent of GDP was consumer spending on imported goods using borrowed money. That, I argued, was not wealth creation as the term *economic growth* implied, but wealth destruction. It was not as though we were importing capital goods to be used to produce consumer goods that could be sold here or abroad for profit. It was consumer goods we were importing, and we were sending the profits over there.

Where I really took heat, though, was on the subject of real estate. Real estate had become a sacred cow, the wholesome driver of the twenty-first century economy. I dared argue that real estate had become a speculative episode of terrifying proportions whose inevitable crash would reach every corner of the economy.

Home equity was fool's gold being mistaken for wealth, I warned, and with 47 percent of the new jobs created in the preceding six years being directly related to home construction, and consumer spending a function of home equity extractions, housing-related wealth effects, and temporarily low teaser rates on adjustable rate mortgages, an entire economy was riding on the obviously naïve assumption that values would rise indefinitely.

Speaking as a minority of one, I predicted then (read *Crash Proof* if you don't believe me) that the subprime market would soon collapse and spread to the general mortgage market and then become an economy-wide credit crisis. I also said inflation would mean crude oil, which I had started buying at less than $20 per barrel and which was around $60 in late 2006, would rise above $100 a barrel and go higher, which has since happened. I called gold, which was around $650 an ounce when my book came out, a "supreme buying opportunity" when others were calling a top. In March 2008, it was flirting with $1,000 an ounce and, I believe, ultimately will head much higher. I predicted that other precious and industrial metals and agricultural commodities would also rise, and they have risen spectacularly. As of this writing, silver and platinum have skyrocketed. Over a 52-week period, soybean prices are up 90 percent and wheat 150 percent.

And I predicted that the dollar would keep plunging. With the euro now worth over half again as much as the dollar, there are shops on New York's Fifth Avenue preferring payment in euros. Euros are also being accepted by retailers in the ultra-chic Hamptons. Others are making it on volume from shoppers who fly over from Italy, take a room at the Hotel Pierre, buy (with cheap dollars) shoes that came from Italy in the first place, fly back, and count their savings. (Even allowing for a little hyperbole, things have gotten that crazy.) It can't last.

If making so much of how accurate my predictions have been seems immodest, let me assure you that bragging rights are not my motive. It's all in the way of establishing credibility so you'll take the predictions and recommendations I make later in this book seriously.

In fact, there is one prediction I made that was wrong, or let's say premature. I said interest rates, which were being kept unsustainably low, thus keeping the real estate bubble inflated and adding to inflation elsewhere, would rise sharply. As I write this, long-term rates are still artificially low, meaning bond prices are artificially high. (In the bond market, prices and yields move in opposite directions). So let me make that prediction again. Bonds are a bubble soon to pop. However, while the government has not seen a significant increase in its borrowing cost, for the private sector it is a completely different story. Mortgage interest rates have already risen, particularly for those with little to put down, low FICO scores, or undocumented incomes, or those seeking jumbo mortgages. These increases will be that much more dramatic once the bond market bubble finally bursts. In addition, corporate borrowing costs have risen, particularly for lower-rated issuers, and credit card rates are rising, as is interest on student loans. More important, not only is private credit getting more expensive, but it is increasingly harder to come by. As to the credit crunch, shell-shocked lenders, saddled with losses on existing debt, have turned off the credit spigots. Home equity lines of credit are being canceled and credit card limits reduced, and the secondary market for nonconforming mortgages and student loans is becoming practically nonexistent.

In any event, I don't think it's brain surgery to predict that a playboy who is without a job and living the high life on credit card debt is going to run into trouble. Why, then, is it not just as obvious that a nation that, *on a chronic basis*, consumes more than it produces; imports the difference, running up huge external liabilities in the process; borrows rather than saves; and spends the borrowed money on nonproductive consumer goods and services, is going to hit the same wall as the playboy?

There is, of course, one huge difference: A nation can create money and the individual cannot. But the more money it prints, the less purchasing power the money will have. The end result for the offending nation will be the destruction of its economy by massive inflation.

———————————— ∾ ————————————

A nation can create money and the individual cannot. But the more money it prints, the less purchasing power the money will have. The end result is our nation will ultimately destroy its economy with inflation.

————————————————————————————

Inflation is on everybody's mind, yet widely misunderstood. This is all the more troublesome as inflation figures so prominently in the escalating economic crisis in nearly all its manifestations. In Chapter 2, I explain how inflation, which to most people is the same as the consumer price index and within safe limits, could so quickly and inconspicuously have become a threat of cataclysmic significance.

The Real Estate Bubble Bursts

The first signs I detected that the real estate bubble was finally leaking air were early in 2007 as homebuilders and mortgage lenders reported disappointing first quarter results and lowered their income projections for the year. However, I first started warning about the bubble itself, and the dire consequences for our economy once it burst, several years before that.

The results reflected, I believe, buyer skittishness prompted by the rise to 5.25 percent in mid-2006 of the federal funds rate, the reference point for mortgages and other interest rates. That was the highest federal funds rate since the real estate boom began, and the reaction gives an indication of just how little it took for an overextended public to go from exuberance to caution. Imagine the reaction, especially when home equity dries up, to a rise in rates sufficient to bring down inflation and put a floor beneath the dollar.

By early spring 2006 the real estate slowdown began to be felt in other areas of the economy, such as capital goods orders, and options and futures prices began anticipating additional stimulative cuts in the federal funds rate.

The most ominous signs, however, were rising default rates in the subprime sector of the mortgage market, which accounted for $600 billion or 20 percent of all mortgages in 2006. These mortgages, nonqualifying for Freddie Mac or Fannie Mae and often made with no down payment, no income documentation, and at teaser rates adjustable at significantly higher reset rates in the future, were arranged by mortgage brokers and then sold off to packagers that pooled and securitized them. The mortgage-backed securities were then repackaged as derivative securities called *collateralized debt obligations* (CDOs) that were structured in ways that got them investment-grade bond ratings. They were then sold directly to banks, hedge funds, and other institutions that were attracted by their high yields, which were a trade-off for their lack of liquidity. The institutions carried them at values based on sophisticated mathematical modeling rather than real supply and demand.

Initially the government and Wall Street dismissed the developing subprime crisis as being contained. However, in a commentary posted on my europac.net web site in March of 2007 entitled "Do Not Uncork the Champagne Just Yet," I wrote, "With the apparent blessing of the Fed, Wall Street can now borrow a page from the Las Vegas promotional playbook and claim that 'what happens in subprime stays in subprime.' Unfortunately, like an out-of-work showgirl with a folder full of embarrassing photos, the problems with subprime will soon show up on everyone's doorstep." Later that year Jim Grant of *Grant's Interest Rate Observer* humorously observed that those who proclaimed that the subprime problems were contained were right only to the extent that the problems were contained to the planet Earth.

It was this kind of default-prone paper that later caused massive write-offs at institutions like Citigroup, which got a $7 billion cash infusion from Abu Dhabi, and Bear Stearns, which was purchased in May 2008 by

JPMorgan Chase with the help of the Federal Reserve. Rather than being contained, subprime problems were just the tip of a huge iceberg, the totality of which has yet to surface even now.

Contrary to Wall Street and government assurances and consistent with my forecast, subprime foreclosures spread into the prime mortgage market, affecting lenders of all types and allied businesses such as bond insurers, government-sponsored entities like Freddie and Fannie, bond-rating agencies, and, not least of all, consumers who have been deprived of the home equity they naively regarded as wealth. As consumers are faced with soaring oil and food costs and now limited to funds available on their credit cards (the next crisis), businesses like The Sharper Image and Linens 'n Things have filed for bankruptcy; airlines are in deep trouble, as are automakers and countless other businesses dependent on consumer credit and travel.

Consumer credit is another meltdown waiting to happen. Delinquencies are on the rise in auto loans, many of which are secured by SUVs and other gas-guzzlers having reduced resale values; student loans, where the tarnishing of traditionally good repayment records is a clear sign of too much borrowing; and credit card debt, which is approaching $1 trillion. Aggressively marketed by issuers charging loan-shark rates, credit cards have become veritable ATMs for people who, with an attitude of impunity, borrow their available credit knowing they can never repay. Perhaps they assume they'll be bailed out like the victims of predatory mortgage lenders, whose loans often paid off credit card debt, but in the meantime their continued spending keeps consumer demand higher than it should be. Like subprime mortgages, credit card, auto loan, and student loan paper is bought and securitized by private firms, eventually becoming asset-backed bonds carried at theoretical values on the books of hedge funds and institutions.

What is now happening in the airline industry is another harbinger of things to come and reflects the lower standard of living that average Americans will be forced to suffer. As the dollar loses value against other currencies, and as citizens of those countries experience rising real incomes relative to Americans, the cost of air transportation relative to incomes will rise sharply in America as it falls elsewhere. As middle-class Chinese, Russians, and Indians take to the skies for the first time, middle-class Americans will be earthbound, as the jet fuel formerly used to power our planes will instead be used to power theirs.

The problem currently confronting our airline industry is not merely that jet fuel prices are too high, but that poorer Americans can no longer afford the higher ticket prices that would enable the airlines to absorb those higher prices. The industry will therefore have to contract to the point where it will be small enough to operate profitably. With fewer planes in the air, airlines will finally have real pricing power, and the resulting sky-high ticket prices will restrict air travel to those wealthy Americans still able to pay the freight. This will pave the way for major expansions of foreign carriers, as wealthier citizens abroad take to the skies in our place.

The concept of demand destruction domestically and demand creation elsewhere, while causing domestic consumer prices to rise to levels that will force malls and big-box retailers to shut down, will actually bring prices down in other cases. College tuitions, kept artificially high as a direct result of the wide availability of student loans, for example, will collapse as the market for such loans evaporates and fewer people attend college.

A Hair of the Dog: Paulson and Bernanke to the Rescue

I do a weekly commentary for clients on my web site, and in February 2008 I wrote one titled "Upping the Inflation Dosage." Referring to the Fed's cutting rates by 325 basis points from 5.25 to 2 percent, and the Bush administration's $150 billion emergency economic "stimulus" package, I said:

> Now that rate cuts alone are proving insufficient, mainly because banks are now so overloaded with

questionable collateral and shaky loans that few can consider acquiring more assets or extending additional credit, the government is opting for a more direct approach. By printing money and mailing it directly to the citizenry, the "stimulus plan" cuts out all the financial middlemen and administers the inflation drug directly to consumers.

I pointed out that mailing checks straight to the taxpayers instead of channeling money through the banking system meant that consumers could bid up consumer prices immediately. This avoids the usual time lag when the Fed's expansions of the money supply, such as the $436 billion injected recently, have to filter through the asset markets before eventually affecting consumer prices. I'm being sarcastic, of course, but the point is valid.

The message, in any event, is that efforts to combat recession through stimulus measures mean more money chasing a given supply of goods. Being the very definition of inflation, that simply pushes up prices while doing nothing to improve underlying economics. It is amazing how Congress can actually pass economic stimulus packages that merely stimulate inflation, and then hold hearings to investigate why oil prices are rising. It adds insult to injury when our government creates a problem and then compounds it by wasting even more taxpayer money trying to determine its cause!

Efforts to combat recession through stimulus measures mean more money chasing a given supply of goods. Being the very definition of inflation, that simply pushes up prices while doing nothing to improve underlying economics.

Nor should taxpayers be cheered by the Fed's announcement that it would swap $200 billion of Treasury debt for $200 billion of mortgage-backed securities owned by Wall Street firms, or its agreement to fund up to $30 billion of Bear Stearns' "less liquid assets" as part of the deal whereby the firm avoided bankruptcy by selling out to JPMorgan Chase. In both instances treasuries are being exchanged for bad paper, and in all likelihood there will more cases like it. In the end, Americans will be on the hook for the losses, either directly through higher taxes or indirectly through more inflation.

The Outlook

The coming decade will witness a radical transformation of the American economy, marked by rising inflation, higher interest rates, and soaring commodity prices, coupled with a weakening dollar; declining markets in stocks, bonds, and real estate; and recession. Asset-based wealth creation and home equity, the cornerstone of the good times during the bubble years, have been revealed as shams, and the economy will have to return to its traditional roots of saving and producing rather than borrowing and consuming.

In my view, there is a real possibility that a new administration in Washington will confront its economic challenges with New Deal–type programs that will only exacerbate the damage and turn the current recession into a repeat of the Great Depression, only with consumer prices rising instead of falling. As I write this in mid-2008, the government still claims the U.S. economy is not in recession. This absurdity is premised on not having two consecutive quarters of negative economic growth, the widely accepted definition of recession. However, with the government determining the GDP and using highly suspect inflation rates with which to adjust the nominal rise (as I explain further in Chapter 3), we may never officially be in a recession. With the automobile, airline, and housing industries in outright collapse and our banking and financial system on government life support, grim reality once again conflicts with government fantasy.

Parting Words

We are entering perilous times—a recession I predict will last well into the next decade and a cataclysmic upheaval of the American way of life as we know it. The bursting of the real estate bubble has made America's fundamental economic problems worse and put us on a course where recession and inflation are inevitable and hyperinflation is a distinct possibility. Various economic stimulus policies of the Fed and the administration may buy some time but will make inflation, which is now an international problem caused by America, a much greater problem. The dollar's decline will continue even though interest rates will inevitably rise.

Therefore a totally nontraditional investment approach is required, which begins with getting out of the United States dollar and into commodities, precious metals, and equities in foreign countries where wealth is growing and currencies are appreciating against the dollar. My goal in writing this book is to share, in detail, my investment approach to help you weather and, yes, even profit from the coming storm.

Chapter Two

Saving Your Assets

— ∽ —

Stay Out of Cash and Bonds

WHEN YOGI BERRA, asked what he thought about the economy, said, "A nickel ain't worth a dime anymore," he seemed at least to intuit that sound money should be a top national priority, a point a lot of people in pinstripes still don't seem to get.

In Chapter 1, I made the case that the dollar's vanishing purchasing power is collapsing the American economy. Here I want to focus on how inflation, which most people think begins and ends with the consumer price index under the watchful eye of the Federal Reserve, is actually created by the same Federal Reserve wearing another hat. The real inflation story should alarm you and help you understand the urgency of my advice.

A Little Background

Our government takes considerable pains to reinforce the misconception that the inflation problem is limited to rising prices well within its control, although the specter of $200-a-barrel oil is making it difficult to defend that fiction. The fact is that rising consumer prices are just a symptom of a root malignancy. The basic problem is being exacerbated daily as the Federal Reserve prints more money to accommodate an administration with a political agenda and no alternative left other than painful recession or worse.

In its terminal phase, inflation becomes hyperinflation, the scourge that collapsed the Weimar Republic in Germany in the early 1920s, Argentina's economy in the early years of the present decade, and Zimbabwe's economy today, and that threatens to ravage the American economy in the not too distant future if present monetary policy is not radically changed.

Hyperinflation has historically been experienced in every society that has used *fiat money*, the term for currency that, like the dollar (since the gold standard was abandoned in 1971), has no intrinsic value. With no restraints and many incentives, the printing presses roll, and eventually currency is devalued to the point where it becomes devoid of purchasing power and practically worthless. (We are not alone, as every other global currency is now fiat money.)

As inflation gets worse, financial assets denominated in the failing currency and the income they throw off become progressively less valuable. Ironically, in times this dire, cash and bonds, which are the time-honored safe havens during stock market crashes, become the worst assets to hold when the dollar is crashing. Cash and cash equivalents simply become increasingly depreciated in value. Bonds, which are really cash payments that are deferred, pay less and less in the current market and will lose capital value if sold before maturity as higher rates cause market prices to decline. I'd reinvest any cash you don't need for walking-around money in a nondollar money market fund or foreign equity portfolios and would unload bonds right now, while rates are still artificially low and prices artificially high. That also goes for Treasury Inflation Protected Securities (TIPS), whose return is adjusted using the CPI, a flawed and inadequate measure of real inflation.

———————————— ∼ ————————————

I'd reinvest any cash you don't need for walking-around money in a nondollar money market fund or foreign equity portfolio and would unload bonds (and TIPS) right now, while rates are still artificially low and prices artificially high.

———————————————————————————

Stocks are a slightly different story and a rather intriguing one at that. Although I expect stocks generally to decline, for both economic and dollar-related reasons, there will be a few that might actually thrive during the collapse and others that, assuming the companies stay in business, can be expected to gain when the economy gets back on its feet. My preference is strongly for foreign equities, of course, but I'll share my ideas about domestic holdings in Chapter 4.

Understanding Inflation

What people have to understand about inflation is that it causes, and is not caused by, rising prices. The word *inflate* means to expand, not to go up or down, and inflation results whenever the money supply and credit are expanded. Prices rise when that expansion occurs without a commensurate expansion of goods and services. Many people declared inflation dead after Fed Chairman Paul

Volcker assaulted it with 20 percent–plus interest rates in the early years of the Reagan administration. It proved to be a lively corpse.

———————————— ≈ ————————————

What people have to understand about inflation is that it causes, and is not caused by, rising prices.

The Federal Reserve, in the past 20 or so years and under the chairmanships of Alan Greenspan and Ben Bernanke, has made it a practice to add liquidity to the economy by increasing the money supply on a regular basis, thus creating invisible inflation over and above what is reported (and understated) in the CPI and its wholesale equivalent, the producer price index (PPI) figures.

The government actually needs inflation to operate the way it does, and, as my father, Irwin Schiff, wrote in his book *The Biggest Con: How the Government Is Fleecing You* (Freedom Books, 1977), it acts as the government's silent partner. The government creates this inflation invisibly by expanding the money supply. Here are the main reasons:

- Inflation is used for political reasons to stimulate the economy and counteract down-cycles that are perfectly normal and corrective of excesses but are unpopular with voters.

- Government debt and other obligations such as social security become more manageable when payable with cheaper dollars.
- Inflated incomes increase government revenues by forcing people into higher tax brackets.
- Inflation helps finance entitlement programs that would otherwise cause tax hikes.

The CPI and PPI, which are prepared by the Department of Labor, report on inflation as it affects typical prices of goods and commodities. But the CPI and PPI are part of the propaganda apparatus. Not only are they largely bogus statistics constructed in a way that understates price increases, but the government represents them as official measures of inflation, ignoring inflation not reflected in consumer or producer prices. By focusing attention on a red herring, the government is deliberately diverting attention away from the real rate of inflation and its role in creating it.

Price versus Systemic Inflation

In no way do the CPI and PPI indexes measure the true extent to which prices are rising as a direct consequence of government-created inflation. They track the prices of a fixed basket of goods bought by a typical consumer or

wholesaler based on a 1982 value of $100. But the formu-
lae used to compute these indexes are creatively adjusted,
using substitutions, geometric weighting, hedonics (productivity science), and other gimmicks. For example, the
inflated price of residential housing was never reflected in
the CPI because instead of using home sales figures, the
Department of Labor substitutes a figure they call "owner
equivalent rent." With all the shenanigans used to turn
renters into buyers during the recent bubble, the rental
market went into a slump for lack of takers. Since owner
equivalent rent was used to represent residential real estate
prices in the CPI, the index significantly understated the
rate at which real estate prices were actually rising.

There is also a distinction made between *core inflation*,
which excludes food and energy prices for the legitimate
reason that their volatility would cause extrapolations to be
misleading, and *headline inflation*. The mischief comes in
when government press releases give greater prominence
to the lower, more comforting, of the two figures. For purposes of smoothing volatility, looking at core prices might
make sense on a monthly basis, but looking at year-over-
year core figures is pointless, as any monthly volatility is
surely smoothed out over the longer time frame. However,
when prices for food and energy rise month after month,
year after year, this is not volatility but a trend the government is simply trying to deny exists.

But total inflation, including what's in the system but not yet reflected in consumer or producer prices, is impossible to measure and can only be estimated. New money enters the system in different ways and at different speeds. Without getting into a discourse on Federal Reserve operations, it expands or contracts the money supply by buying or selling government securities in the open market or by using other techniques that affect commercial banks' ability or incentive to lend. When it expands the money supply, we use a kind of shorthand and say it is "printing money."

When the government prints money, ultimately diminishing the purchasing power of each dollar already in circulation, it is also reducing the value of assets, such as stocks, real estate, and other assets measured in dollars. When an economy is significantly pervaded by inflation, as ours is, it is important but difficult, since systemic inflation can't be measured, to compare investment values on an inflation-adjusted basis.

The concept of inflation remains fairly elusive: Since the real rate can't be quantified, we have to compare changes in *nominal* prices to price changes in a commodity, such as gold, which is a better store of value and therefore a more objective standard by which to measure prices. Ratios representing these price relationships have historically guided us in judging how much inflation is reflected in nominal prices.

~

The concept of inflation remains fairly elusive: Since the real rate can't be quantified, we have to compare changes in *nominal* prices to price changes in a commodity, such as gold, which is a better store of value and therefore a more objective standard by which to measure prices.

So we wind up, for example, saying the Dow Jones Industrial Average was up *x* percent in nominal terms; but priced in gold or in other commodities, it was really up or down by *y* percent in real or inflation-adjusted terms. Still, it is vitally important that best estimates be figured into our financial judgments and the way we evaluate performance.

Exported Inflation

Inflation, as noted in an earlier example, may also be exported. Imported goods are paid for with inflated dollars that accumulate abroad, thus overhanging but not immediately affecting the domestic economy. By *overhanging*, I mean dollars held by foreign central banks are IOU-nothings redeemable for what they might be worth in American goods, services, or assets.

With the dollar's domestic purchasing power steadily declining, the risk looms ever larger that foreign holders will redeem (spend) their accumulated IOUs in the country that issued them. The consequences of their doing so en masse are potentially very serious.

If foreign holders use their dollars to buy American companies, as is being done increasingly through sovereign wealth funds, earnings streams vital to the American economy are diverted to foreign owners, as is the political influence they represent. If they are spent in the American marketplace (either on existing goods they produced and exported to us in the first place, or on stuff we produced ourselves), foreign dollars compete with domestic dollars and send prices soaring.

~

If foreign holders use their dollars to buy American companies, as is being done increasingly through sovereign wealth funds, earnings streams vital to the American economy are diverted to foreign owners, as is the political influence they represent. If they are spent in the American marketplace, foreign dollars compete with domestic dollars and send prices soaring.

In another sense, American inflation is being exported as foreign governments adjust their currencies to prevent them from gaining too much value against the dollar. Such adjustments are also made where foreign currencies are pegged to the dollar, as is the case in the Middle East and China, where inflation is rampant, and in other emerging economies. (Note: China now has a so-called soft peg where the rise of its renminbi, or RMB, which is also called the yuan, is managed.) The removal of these dollar pegs would greatly increase the standard of living in countries where pegs exist, while simultaneously reducing the dollar's value and the standard of living here in America.

Ironically, the financial media once again have it completely backwards, as the rising price of imported goods is referred to as "our importing inflation from abroad." This, of course, misses the point entirely, as those prices are in fact only rising as a direct result of all the money being printed abroad to buy up all the dollars we used to pay for our imports. It is not America importing inflation, but the inflation chickens we exported coming home to roost. Also, referring to inflation as being "imported" takes the Fed off the hook, and the government can claim that prices are rising due to forces completely beyond its control. As the Church Lady use to say, "How convenient."

Of course, the government concocts all sorts of villains and scapegoats for the inflation it creates. As I write this chapter, Congress is considering a ban on oil futures trading, as rising oil prices are being attributed to speculators. Of course, blaming speculators for higher oil prices is a complete farce, and is analogous to blaming the rain on people carrying umbrellas. The ultimate irony is that in the absence of speculators, whose actions facilitate hedging and send important price signals to producers, oil prices would be even higher. So if the government succeeds at stopping speculation, not only will oil prices continue to rise as a result of central bank money creation, but those increases will be even greater as a result of the added costs imposed on producers by removing speculators from the market. In other words, it will be a typical government program, where the legislation worsens the very problem it purports to solve.

Further, the fact that the government has the nerve to blame inflation on rising commodity prices is the ultimate in chutzpa. It's analogous to someone stuffing his face with junk food, never exercising, and then blaming the scale for his obesity. The key point to remember is that as more dollars are created, thus diminishing the value of each one, more are required to buy a given quantity of goods. Many on Wall Street try to dismiss the obvious connection between the dollar's value and commodity prices by pointing out that the rise in commodity prices exceeds the rate of the dollar's decline. The problem with this observation, however, is that it compares the dollar's value to that of other fiat currencies that are also losing value. The fact is that all currencies, including the euro, are losing value—it's just that the dollar is losing value faster. As a result, prices are rising in all currencies, just at different rates. A truer measure would be to price commodities in gold.

Another popular scapegoat, one that also allows the government to claim that inflation is beyond its control, is strong economic growth abroad, especially in emerging markets such as China and India. However, that dog won't hunt either, as it ignores the tremendous increase in output that is the true source of that growth. As more goods are produced, particularly agricultural commodities due to greatly enhanced farm productivity, prices should be falling. The only reason they are not is because money supply is growing even faster. True economic growth causes prices to fall. It's the growth in money supply that causes them to rise.

Of course the Fed talks tough about its resolve to fight inflation, and Wall Street buys the rhetoric hook, line, and sinker. It carefully dissects the language of its statements and the minutes of its meetings, to discern the degree and timing of future rate hikes to put teeth in its rhetoric. Yet despite its inflation bark, the Fed will never bite. Rather than paying close attention to what it says, Wall Street should instead watch what it actually does. Actions always speak louder than words, and the Fed's actions, or lack thereof, are deafening. It's analogous to your overweight friend constantly talking about the diets he plans to start or the gyms he intends to join, while reclining in an easy chair in front of the boob tube with a beer in one hand and a Twinkie in the other.

The Bretton Woods Agreements of 1944

It is impossible to understand the background of the present economic crisis without understanding what was accomplished at Bretton Woods.

The Bretton Woods conference of 1944 produced a plan to fix the rate of exchange for all currencies in Europe and Asia in relation to the United States dollar, which, in turn, would be tied to gold to permit international settlement at a fixed price. A unit of foreign currency would thus be exchangeable for a fixed number of dollars, and a set number of dollars would be exchangeable for an ounce of gold.

International gold backing, until the Nixon administration ended it and went from a fixed to a floating exchange rate in 1971, had limited the Federal Reserve's ability to print money and create inflation. To maintain confidence in the dollar, the Fed had to be conscious of the ratio of dollars to reserves, meaning it couldn't add freely to the money supply without adding to the gold reserves. But Nixon was facing huge budget deficits from the Johnson administration guns and butter policies in the late 1960s—the Vietnam War, the Great Society programs, the war on poverty, and the space race with Soviet Russia—and had used the money-creating powers of the Federal Reserve to the point where countries abroad were forced to expand their money supplies at the same rate to maintain agreed-upon ratios of their currencies to the dollar. We were exporting inflation, and some European and Asian countries began presenting dollars for redemption in gold. Nixon saw no alternative but to close the international gold window.

&

International gold backing, until the Nixon administration ended it and went from a fixed to a floating exchange rate in 1971, had limited the Federal Reserve's ability to print money and create inflation.

The United States dollar, having lost its domestic gold backing in 1963, was, after 1971, what is called a *fiat currency*, meaning it had no intrinsic value whatsoever. It had become, as my father called it in his book *The Biggest Con*, an IOU nothing—a piece of paper whose only value was its purchasing power, which in turn depended on the strength of the economy and the way monetary policy affected the money supply.

In fact, in 1968, during congressional hearings related to the removal of gold backing from Federal Reserve notes, my father, an insurance agent from New Haven, Connecticut, testified that doing so would lead to a precipitous decline in the value of the dollar, rising inflation, the misguided imposition of wage and price controls, and a surge in the price of gold. In sharp contrast, government expert witnesses such as Senator William Proxmire of Wisconsin, the chairman of the Senate Banking Committee; Henry H. Fowler, the Secretary of the Treasury; and William McChesney Martin Jr., chairman of the Federal Reserve, all testified that removing gold backing would actually strengthen the dollar and lead to lower gold prices. My father's complete testimony as well as excerpts from government witnesses were reproduced as appendixes in his book *The Biggest Con*.

Within months of the passage of the legislation in 1971, there were runs on the dollar in Europe, and the dollar's exchange value against other currencies had plunged by about 70 percent by 1978. Gold prices, set at $35 per ounce at the time of the hearings, surged to $850 by 1980. Nixon imposed wage and price controls in August of 1971 and then removed them in April of 1974.

Government experts, who basically argued that a dollar backed by nothing was better than a dollar backed by something, could not have been more wrong, while an obscure insurance agent from New Haven nailed it perfectly. It is ironic that today those very experts (same titles, different names) are again making the same rosy predictions based on misguided economic stimulus payments and government bailouts, while the son of that insurance agent and author of this book sounds the alarm.

The Dollar's Reserve Currency Status

Another development of critical importance to our current situation that came out of the Bretton Woods accords was the designation of the United States dollar as the world's reserve currency. This meant that the dollar became the currency used by other governments and institutions as a major part of their foreign exchange reserves and as the international pricing currency for products traded on global markets, such as oil and gold.

The significance of reserve currency status, which we still enjoy, however precariously, is that unless other nations take positive action to force adjustment, we can postpone having to balance our trade account. If we were to lose our reserve status (and there is always talk about replacing it with the euro or some combination of foreign currencies), the free market would force a devaluation of the dollar to bring our account into balance. That would be the equivalent of forcing an out-of-control vehicle to stop on a dime. All the standard-of-living adjustments we have been talking about as being inevitable over a period of years would be forced immediately on an unready American population.

The Significance of Decoupling

Decoupling? Coupling sounds like fun, but decoupling?

Decoupling is a clumsy word whose meaning derives from *coupling,* the term that became part of the economics vocabulary when it was believed that globalization would result in such interdependence among world economies that problems in one would necessarily become problems in the rest. Since the United States was the leading economic power until recently, the fear was that any problems here would spread worldwide. If the United States sneezes, the conventional wisdom holds that the rest of the world catches a cold.

The good news is that, although our recent credit problems have been felt in markets abroad, it is no longer true that America's economic maladies will affect in any basic or permanent way the vitality of other developed economies. The fact that even in a global economy, sovereign countries can have self-sufficient economies offering finance and investment opportunities immune to the ailments of other nations, is an accepted reality. There are many naysayers, but I have built a successful business around the slogan "There's a bull market somewhere."

I have followed my strategy of investing in foreign equities personally and have done very well.

I'm rather fond of the word *decoupling*, in fact, because it fits two of my favorite analogies. The first is that America is no longer the engine of world economic growth but rather the caboose. When the caboose is decoupled from the train, the engine—now the producing economies primarily of Asia—will pick up speed and represent even greater investment opportunity for Americans smart enough to seize it. The other is that our relationship with the world is analogous to the one I had with my former wife. I had a job and earned money, which she promptly spent. My job was not a function of my wife's willingness to spend money; her ability to spend was a function of my ability to earn. Once we decoupled, I could spend my earnings on myself, even though my ex got a property settlement. When China divorces us, the Chinese will keep 100 percent of their property and their factories, use their products themselves, and enjoy a dramatically improved lifestyle. America, like my ex, will have to scale back her lifestyle in line with her production. (In fairness to my ex, she was not really that extravagant, but it's the analogy that's important.)

It is our good fortune, as America's economic problems worsen, that decoupling is a reality and provides an opportunity to preserve and enhance our wealth with nondollar investments while the American economy restructures itself and, in time, it is hoped, becomes the next great investment opportunity.

Parting Words

I hope I have succeeded in giving you an understanding of what inflation really means and what causes it, and of the catastrophic situation that will exist if the debasement of the dollar continues. The Federal Reserve has worked itself into the uncomfortable position of being between a rock and a hard place. If it continues its policy of economic stimulation by increasing inflation, we risk hyperinflation and eventual collapse. If it raises interest rates to bring inflation down, protect the dollar, and preserve foreign investment, it will cause deepening recession in a nation overextended with personal and government debt. It is a choice the incoming administration will have to face, but there is no alternative to sacrifice in one form or another.

However it plays out, the dollar's decline will continue, and the only way to avoid serious loss is to make nondollar-denominated investments before that decline turns into a rout. Get out of cash and bonds right now.

Chapter Three

Beware of False Prophets

~

How Prophets Cost Profits

ECONOMISTS are always ripe targets for the friendly needle, and as I start this chapter an oldie comes to mind. Paradox: When none of the economic theories are working, all the economists are.

I bring that up for levity but also to make a point in defense of economists. Economics may or may not be a dismal science, but it's important to recognize that it is not a natural science, like physics or mathematics, where everything is about facts and outcomes can be predicted with certainty. Economics is a social science where facts are weighed along with questions about how people will act on those facts. That makes a variety of outcomes possible, and explains why economists sometimes seem pusillanimous. However, in the case of those economists who subscribe to popular schools of thought, such as Keynesianism, monetarism, or supply-side, they have left the realm of science altogether, and at best operate within the realm of science fiction. True economics, now referred to as Austrian economics, is seen as a fringe theory, the province of gold bugs and gloom-and-doomers like yours truly. Of course, as my father once said, Austrian economics makes about as much sense as Chinese physics. It's a science, and its laws function the same way no matter where they operate or who attempts to apply them.

In any event, I'd rather see the needle jabbed at the professionals in finance, investment, government, and business generally, who take selected statistics from economists and use them to impart scientific certitude to their own self-serving advice and prognostications.

My goal in this chapter is to share some insights regarding the *agendas* of the different professional groups that lead opinion on questions of economics and investments. If you know where they're coming from, you'll know where to sprinkle the proverbial grains of salt. And you'll have the wherewithal to form your own opinions.

Let's round up the usual suspects.

Usual Suspect 1: Uncle Sam

Our own federal government, meaning the administration and bureaucracy as well as the purportedly independent Federal Reserve, pulls the wool over the public's eyes as a matter of standard operating procedure.

It's true, of course, that confidence and good morale are part of what keeps societies healthy and economies robust, and government officials shouldn't be criticized for having an attitude, metaphorically speaking, that all babies are cute. Nor should officials be tolerated who create fear and anxiety where it is unwarranted. But somewhere in there is a line that, when crossed, has a counterproductive result. It has to do with the public's right to the knowledge it needs to vote intelligently and make sound judgments at the personal level.

Our government has crossed that line, in my opinion, and here are a few examples.

Misrepresenting Inflation

In Chapter 2, I described how the Federal Reserve uses monetary policy—that is, prints money—to finance entitlement programs, to manage debt, to stimulate phony economic growth, and to advance other agendas, thereby creating inflation and debasing the dollar without anybody knowing what's really going on.

The motive for choosing to print money is purely political. The other way to do it would be to raise taxes, which would cause a public uproar costing elected officials their jobs. Not that the voters would stand for any reduction in social programs. The voters want it both ways, and the elected politicians have found a way to accomplish that.

An indication of how secret the Fed wants its money printing activities to be was revealed in 2006. The government had for years been releasing money supply figures, one category of which enabled period-to-period comparisons of money in circulation. Fearing knowledgeable analysts would use that information to determine the amount of inflation being created, the government announced that the category containing it, called M-3, would no longer be made public.

The deception here, as noted earlier, is the government's failure to acknowledge that any inflation exists other than what is reflected in the consumer price index (CPI), a metric whose computation methodology was specifically redesigned so that when it was computed by the Department of Labor, rampant inflation would appear to be relatively contained.

The Labor Department then takes that headline number, which is 4 percent as this is written, and subtracts energy and food components to eliminate distortions that their volatility would otherwise cause in extrapolations. The resulting figure is called *core inflation*. So far, so good. But then the lower core inflation, currently an innocuous 2.2 percent, is trumpeted to mislead the public into thinking that inflation is not a problem. Of course it is a big problem. Real inflation is actually reducing the dollar's purchasing power at an annual rate estimated at between 8 and 10 percent.

That real inflation is a root cause of our economic crisis is something I hope I've by now impressed on you. But to appreciate how it affects our daily choices, consider this example: On May 23, 2008, the Dow Jones Industrial Average closed at 12,480, off 11.4 percent from its October 12, 2007 high of 14,093. That was a bit of a downer for those who thought the Dow was on its way to 16,000, but not bad considering the havoc wreaked by the subprime meltdown. And compared with the previous market cycle high on January 14, 2000, of 11,722, the Dow was still ahead, although not by much. The May 2008 close of 12,480 reflected a gain of 757 points or about 6.5 percent over the eight-year period.

But I've been talking nominal values. If you adjust for inflation at an annual rate of 8 percent (conservative, since estimates range to 10 percent or higher), the Dow over the eight-year period since 2000 lost 4,981 points or some 42 percent of its value. That's a lot of wealth lost. Imagine how Wall Street's routine touting of domestic stocks would look if presented in the context of those facts.

———————————— ∿ ————————————

If you adjust for inflation at an annual rate of 8 percent (conservative, since estimates range to 10 percent or higher), the Dow over the eight-year period since 2000 lost 4,981 points or some 42 percent of its value. That's a lot of wealth lost. Imagine how Wall Street's routine touting of domestic stocks would look if presented in the context of those facts.

———————————————————————————————

The GDP

The gross domestic product (GDP) is the way our government purports to measure economic growth and wealth creation. We're approaching 2009 as I write this, and we hear stories about people who can't afford the gas to look for work that would save their homes from foreclosure. But not to worry: As long as the GDP keeps growing, we won't have to worry about the "R" word. A recession is defined as two consecutive quarters of negative GDP growth.

What makes the GDP grow? Any exchange of goods or services for money within the borders of the United

States increases the GDP and, in this sense, appears to create wealth. When former New York governor Elliott Spitzer made a highly publicized trip to Washington that he would rather forget, he at least increased the GDP, rather significantly by most reports.

Earlier this year a series of tornados and floods destroyed billions of dollars of wealth in the Midwest. But wealth destroyed doesn't subtract anything from the GDP. In fact, any money spent cleaning up, rebuilding, and paying for hospital care in the aftermath of such disasters actually adds to GDP. Obviously society would be much better off had nothing been destroyed and scarce resources not been diverted to repair the damage.

Then there is the money borrowed from foreign sources and spent here on imported TVs and other non-productive goods, which adds to the GDP and counts as economic growth and wealth creation when actually it has the opposite effect.

The only subtraction from GDP numbers are inflation adjustments using, of course, the government's own bogus measures. By understating inflation, the government automatically overstates GDP and effectively manufactures economic growth out of thin air. In addition, much of what is included in GDP is padded with hedonics (discussed next, under productivity) and full of all sorts of fluff.

The importance of seeing through this artifice is that we are making decisions based on it. Uncle Sam is using GDP growth as evidence that a weak, dangerously over-extended economy is strong, healthy, and growing, and that Americans should therefore keep spending.

~

Uncle Sam is using GDP growth as evidence that a weak, dangerously overextended economy is strong, healthy, and growing, and that Americans should therefore keep spending.

Often when I argue with fellow pundits on television or radio, I am accused of wanting to ignore the facts simply because I dismiss government statistics. However, the truth is it's my opponents who ignore reality when they place their faith in government statistics that defy common sense. When it comes to government-contrived facts, also consider the source and the motives of those compiling them. More important, do not base your investment decisions on any government numbers.

Because they believe the government, people are buying stocks that are really going down but that due to underreported inflation appear to be going up. But how can those people be expected to think in terms of real

BEWARE OF FALSE PROPHETS   [51]

versus nominal values when the very existence of inflation is being denied?

Americans watch their national debt mount into unrepayable trillions of dollars, but don't get particularly concerned about it because experts tell them "as a percentage of GDP, the debt by historical standards is not excessive."

I could go on, but you get the picture. We're sick enough to be sweating through our pajamas, but the government thermometer reads 98.6 degrees. There's obviously something wrong with the thermometer.

Productivity

The panacea ballyhooed for just about all of our economic problems is our so-called increased productivity resulting from modern technology. This is another example of government propaganda.

Productivity gains are a real thing, don't get me wrong, but the question here is twofold: In the overall balance of things, how important a factor has higher productivity really been? And if it is true that we are more productive than our trading partners, why is our trade deficit widening, not shrinking?

The fact is that productivity gains have been grossly exaggerated by the statisticians specializing in the field known as *hedonics*. In one notable and ironic case, they did it by devising a creative formula for measuring the contribution of computers. Productivity measures the amount of consumer goods a business is capable of producing in a given amount of time. If a computer manufacturer produces a new computer with 10 times the power of the computer it replaces, the creative formula used by hedonics analysts multiplies the productivity of the manufacturer by 10, creating an absurd distortion. The fact that the computer has 10 times the power is not only irrelevant, it doesn't multiply anything by 10 except, of course, the statistic. If my new laptop is 10 times as fast as my old one, am I 10 times as productive after buying it? Not unless I learn to type 10 times faster.

If, however, the more powerful computer is purchased by a business, rendering it a capital good, productivity is not measured by how productive the tool is but by how its utilization affects the output of consumer goods. Only if productivity of consumer goods increases tenfold can we say that the computer, which itself might be 10 times faster then the model it replaced, has increased user productivity by a factor of 10!

While we'll continue to hear a lot of talk about productivity gains, the American economy will continue to produce less, and the number of unemployed Americans will continue to grow.

I wrote a commentary on productivity some time back and concluded that a company increases productivity by simply replacing domestic labor with less expensive foreign labor. The savings for America is greatly reduced as the so-called added productivity comes at the expense of a growing current account deficit. So, while we'll continue to hear a lot of talk about productivity gains, the American economy will continue to produce less, and the number of unemployed Americans will continue to grow.

Unemployment

Speaking of which, unemployment numbers are yet another example of the government's efforts to gild the economic lily.

The government provides monthly figures on non-farm payrolls and unemployment, which is 5.5 percent as this is being written. That figure is worrisome, especially because it is increasing, but it is still low enough by historical standards for presidential candidate John McCain to tick it off as one of the indications that the United States economy is fundamentally very strong.

My problem with unemployment numbers is that they exclude the long-term unemployed—people working part-time when they prefer to work full-time; others who, because they cannot find jobs, opt for self-employment but have little in the way of real earnings; discouraged workers; and any unemployed people not actively seeking jobs.

How in the world can that be explained except as a way to understate the problem? But why? What does the government have to gain by giving the public phony unemployment figures? The answer is obvious: They want you to think things are better than they really are.

———————— ∼ ————————

What does the government have to gain by giving the public phony unemployment figures? The answer is obvious: They want you to think things are better than they really are.

Usual Suspect 2: Wall Street

Wall Street, as I use the term, refers to investment banking and brokerage firms, mutual funds, and the relatively new but hugely rich and somewhat furtive hedge fund industry.

Investment Banks

The propaganda question looms largest in the investment banking/brokerage segment and arises from inherent conflicts of interest.

Simplistically stated, these firms are in the business of *underwriting* stocks and bonds for a corporate clientele and providing *brokerage* services for a retail clientele. Obviously they have many other activities, such as providing investment advisory services to wealthy customers, advising on corporate mergers and acquisitions, doing securities analysis and research, and much more. (Until recently, a number of them made a killing buying subprime mortgages and securitizing them for resale to institutional clients. Of course the tables turned, and now the subprime mortgage adventure is killing them. But that's another story.)

But the basic conflict of interest (and please understand that to say there is a conflict of interest is not to say it is necessarily abused) is between the underwriting and brokerage functions of firms that do both. An underwriter buys stock from a corporate issuer at one price and then resells it for what it will fetch in the marketplace, through its own and other retail brokerage operations. The potential conflict is in the relationship between the investment banker and the corporate client on one hand, and on the other, the responsibility the firm has to sell its retail customers a prudent and suitable investment.

In the most obvious instances of abuse, the underwriter might push a lousy stock on its retail customers to ensure the issue sells out and the corporate client is happy. Or the investment bank might overrate its corporate client's stock in a research report so the stock will have a higher market value.

In an example stemming from the recent credit crunch, UBS Investment Bank was named in a suit alleging it defrauded investors in its dual role as underwriter of auction-rate preferred shares (ARPS) and manager of the auctions that set their prices. The ARPS are issued by municipalities, funds, and other institutions and bought by corporations and wealthy individuals as short-term money market instruments that are typically rolled over at dividend rates set at auctions held every seven weeks. When the credit markets seized in August 2007, corporations began to sell their ARPS, putting UBS in the position of finding new buyers or being stuck with the securities. The complaint alleges that UBS, already reeling from subprime mortgage losses, foisted the securities off on innocent public investors to limit its exposure by continuing to represent them as ultrasafe cash equivalents.

Apart from violations of securities laws, however, firms clearly have an interest in a buoyant stock market and, more than that, have the ability and influence to raise public confidence by making positive noises about the market's prospects whether economic and market fundamentals warrant optimism or not.

Even if these firms don't yield to the temptation to whip the public into a bullish mood, they can do harm by not discouraging customer enthusiasm where they know it isn't warranted. I firmly believe Wall Street deserved much more criticism than it got for its failure to discourage investors who bought into the dot-com craze in the 1990s, especially after it became clear to people in the business that the bubble was unsustainable.

This same proclivity to reinforce positive sentiment at the market level has influenced investors' understanding of the relative risk of different types of stocks and of stocks versus bonds.

It's my view, for example, that growth stocks—stocks that reinvest earnings as a way of financing growth and ultimately enhancing share values—are inherently more speculative than stocks that pay out earnings in dividends. It's an extreme example, but the Enron debacle couldn't have happened if the company had a dividend policy that, in effect, forced them to prove their earnings were real.

That bonds are safer than stocks—in other words, that creditors who hold a legal contract are more likely to get their money back if a company fails than are owners—is axiomatic and the reason investors should pay more for a dollar of interest than for a dollar of earnings. Wall Street, though, has conditioned the public to believe that the long-term capital gains potential of stocks is as dependable as bond interest and far more rewarding.

--- ~ ---

The basic agenda of Wall Street investment banks, indeed their raison d'être, is to sell stocks and keep their corporate clients happy. Remember that, and discount the value of their public predictions accordingly.

Hence the formula most commonly used for an individual investment plan: Subtract your age from 100 and use the result as the percentage of your portfolio you should allocate for stocks, allocating the rest to bonds. You're 20? Put 80 percent in stocks, 20 percent in bonds. When you're 70, 30 percent will be stocks, 70 percent bonds. That's fine if you assume. You're assuming stocks always rise, are always appropriately priced relative to valuation, and always have a market waiting when you're ready to sell; and that when you do sell, bonds can be bought that pay you enough to retire on.

I'm not so sure I'd want to be that person retiring right now. Stocks, as we saw earlier, are off 42 percent in real terms from 2000 and bonds are still selling at artificially high prices and paying artificially low yields, the next bubble to burst.

The basic agenda of Wall Street investment banks, indeed their raison d'être, is to sell stocks and keep their corporate clients happy. Remember that, and discount the value of their public predictions accordingly.

Mutual Funds

The agenda of actively managed (as opposed to indexed) mutual funds, including open-end as well as exchange-traded funds (ETFs), is to outperform their competitors on a quarterly basis.

At best, this gives a short-term focus to their trading activities and militates against the time-honored formula for successful investing: patience and discipline. So most of them underperform the market long-term, partly because of the fees they charge, but also because that short-term trading focus, combined with huge portfolios that are limited to stocks with capitalizations high enough to fit in them, forces them to buy overpriced stocks and even to resort to speculation.

Just remember that their agenda and your agenda are probably at some variance. You want absolute long-term performance. They're in a horse race that rewards short-term gains.

But as long as funds are competitive on a quarterly basis, they'll sell shares and represent an influential segment of market and economic opinion. Just remember that their agenda and your agenda are probably at some variance. You want absolute long-term performance. They're in a horse race that rewards short-term gains.

Hedge Funds

Unless you're a pretty fat cat yourself, you are probably not a hedge fund investor, although the industry is always trying to broaden its market using dubious tactics to get past accredited investor rules. The most common example is the fund of funds, where a garden-variety fund operates as a holding company for hedge funds but can exempt its own shareholders from net worth and income requirements.

Be that as it may, hedge funds do have strict wealth requirements but are otherwise largely unregulated and not subject to the disclosure requirements of other funds. I bring them up here because they are a fairly new presence in the marketplace, control trillions of dollars, have already figured in potentially destabilizing scandals and bankruptcies, and, for better or worse, promise to be in the news for a while.

What you need to know about hedge funds is that while many are well managed and use their expertise, financing, and operational freedom constructively, too many are using investors' money to take risks the same investors wouldn't willingly take themselves—risks that are magnified by leverage and not shared equally by hedge fund managers, who take 20 percent of profits with no financial responsibility for losses. In other words, hedge fund managers can make risky bets for years, taking 20 percent of the profits along the way, but in the end, when their bets ultimately go bad and the investors lose most or all of their money, the managers do not have to return any of their excessive fees, which in hindsight they never really deserved to be paid.

Providing an even greater incentive to gamble, the performance fees are paid on what is known as a carried interest, which means an equity stake for which the manager does not put up any of his own capital. As such, these fees are taxed as if they were capital gains and not ordinary income—which they clearly are. Not only does this mean hedge fund managers pay lower income taxes on their incentive fees than on their management fees, but they also escape any FICA taxes as well. This would be an even greater windfall if Barack Obama becomes president and follows through with his pledge to eliminate the earnings cap on Social Security taxes. Of course, the tax treatment of carried interest is now a political hot potato, but lavish political donations from the hedge fund and private equity community have thus far preserved the loophole.

The bottom line is that for a variety of reasons, hedge fund managers have powerful incentives to take risks and leverage them and—note this—to make the same bets in the same markets, meaning that misjudgments can have potentially unthinkable consequences, from which the managers are themselves protected. The investments Bear Stearns' hedge fund subsidiaries made in collateralized debt obligations backed by subprime mortgages are an example we will probably see repeated in other hedge fund collapses. It's interesting that the government is now prosecuting two managers of these funds, claiming they misled investors. The irony, of course, is that the very names of these funds—"High Grade Structured Credit Strategies Fund" and "High Grade Structured Credit Strategies Enhanced Leverage Fund"—and the known fact that the securities being structured and leveraged were high-risk subprime mortgages should have been warning enough. Therefore those supposedly sophisticated investors foolish enough to have invested in these funds got exactly what they deserved. Remember, these funds were created after the real estate bubble had already burst and the problems in the subprime sector were already evident. It seems to me that Bear Stearns laid its cards right on the table, and investors willingly bet on what was obviously a losing hand.

Of course, the ultimate irony is that the government actually has the audacity to prosecute anyone for misleading investors, when practically every economic statistic it compiles is designed to do precisely that.

Hedge funds loom as a potentially destabilizing element in the economy. Nobody really knows what exposures they have, and predictions of economic recovery that don't allow for the hedge fund factor should not be given credibility.

Usual Suspect 3: Industry Groups

Industry and trade association spokespersons are probably too obvious a source of propaganda to warrant discussion here, but they create a lot of headlines by posing as authorities instead of the advocates they really are.

In recent months, of course, the driver of economic calamity has been the real estate industry, a bubble suddenly burst and the catalyst for foreclosures, lost jobs, failed banks, emergency government actions, Wall Street write-offs, unsettled foreign markets, and much that hasn't happened yet. It is as good an example as any to make my point.

When the media look for statistics and Congress seeks professional input, it is invariably the industry itself to which both turn. From industry's perspective however, a mountain is always being made of a molehill. Selected evidence can be very persuasive. You can bet that some-where in today's newspaper there's an article announcing that the market bottom has arrived and anybody who doesn't buy now is missing the opportunity of a lifetime. The article in all likelihood will reference an industry trade group and have statistics that absolutely prove this claim, drawn from the mystical real estate realm of loca-tion, location, and location.

One thing that strikes me as particularly comical is the way the media constantly ask the experts (typically realtors) if the time is right for buyers to step into the market and scoop up the supposed bargains. In the first place, has anyone ever met a realtor who told them now is *not* the time to buy? In the second place, the question misses the point that practically all potential buyers have already bought. There are not too many of us who waited out the bubble, and those of us who did will certainly not be foolish enough to overpay now.

$\sim$

Industry groups are invaluable sources of data but bring a bias to the dialog that should be discounted for what it is.

Sources like me who have studied the problem com-prehensively and objectively and put real estate figures together with other economic realities understand that, were the real estate bubble to reinflate in response to industry happy talk and government economic stimulation, the current economic crisis would only magnify. The only sane course is to allow real estate prices to adjust downward and for Americans to face reality and endure a lower standard of living. This is the only way we can transition back to a viable economy where the values of saving and producing are recognized as essential to prosperity.

The lesson is that industry groups are invaluable sources of data but bring a bias to the dialog that should be discounted for what it is.

Parting Words

We are at a critical crossroads and much hangs on the decisions we make regarding our own finances as well as our elected officials. We have no choice but to listen to advice, but as I have tried to show in this chapter, advice must be carefully evaluated.

The most authoritative sources of advice, such as government leaders, Wall Street professionals, and experts speaking from the industries figuring most largely in the dialog, probably have axes to

(*continued*)

grind. A healthy skepticism of what they say, based on knowledge of their agendas, will force you to get guidance from different sources.

Economists, especially those not on the payrolls of the government, Wall Street, or interested industrial groups, are trying to make the same objective judgments you are, presumably with more knowledge and more advanced skills. Listen to them also, and when they disagree, use your own judgment. In a world where the old rules don't apply, what other choice do you really have?

Chapter Four

Of Babies
and Bathwater

~

*What to Do with My
U.S. Investments*

WITH THE DOLLAR in free fall, holding dollar-denominated cash and bonds, as I said in Chapter 2, puts your wealth in the same free fall, and makes it imperative that you move your dollars into gold, silver, or investments denominated in other currencies. But how about domestic equity investments? Aren't stocks supposed to be inflation proof? Is it necessary to jettison a whole portfolio and replace it with foreign stocks? My unequivocal answer is yes—and no.

The fact is that stocks, unlike cash and bonds, which have no intrinsic value, represent ownership of assets—real stuff—and therefore have some value, assuming the issuing company remains viable and there is some kind of market in which the assets can be exchanged for value. Of course, that value will change for better or worse as the economic crisis plays out.

In the final chapter, I share my thoughts on how the global economic drama may unfold and the scenarios I see possible as the United States gets ahold of itself and begins to rebuild. It would be impossible at this point to sketch out an investment plan for domestic equities, although somewhere in the course of events it should become possible to identify undervalued United States companies destined to profit from the revival I'm confident will ultimately occur.

With very few exceptions, I would strongly recommend that knowledgeably selected foreign stocks, many of which are currently cheap because of the temporary market weakness caused by the upheaval here, replace your domestic portfolio holdings at least for the next three to five years. This is true even though some United

States stocks, such as domestic oil producers and oil service companies, should do very well. The United States in hard times has a way of biting the hand that feeds it, such as imposing excess profit taxes on its most successful companies. Foreign oil producers are less likely to face such problems.

Be that as it may, you may have personal considerations, such as the timing of capital gains, that will influence you to stay in United States stocks, assuming it's relatively safe to do so. My purpose in this chapter is to help you decide which American equities are likely to fare best, and which worst, in the foreseeable environment.

The Current United States Stock Market

The current stock market, as I pointed out earlier, is down 11 percent from where it was at the turn of the century in nominal terms measured by the Dow Jones Industrial Average, but down some 42 percent over the same period adjusted for estimated real rates of inflation. Other indexes, such as the NASDAQ, have fared much worse.

The fact that most people don't make the inflation adjustment is a reflection of the government's success in convincing the public that inflation is negligible, but that's beginning to change. In the first half of 2008, the nominal Dow was off some 6 percent for the year to date, and all indications were that the storm clouds gathering over the economy were being felt in a market that up to then had been in confusion and uncertainty.

The outlook for the American stock market has never looked grimmer, as deepening recession accompanied by higher interest rates and rising raw material costs depresses corporate earnings, and high inflation eats away at the purchasing power of people lucky enough to have jobs.

Generally, the downside for the first half of 2008 was led by the financials, reflecting the battering resulting from the subprime mortgage debacle; industries most directly affected by high gasoline prices, such as airlines and autos; or retailers affected by weaker domestic consumer spending. Stocks leading the upside were exporters, which sell more when the dollar is cheap; the big multinationals, which do a large part of their business abroad and benefit from foreign currency conversion; and commodity-based companies, such as oil and gas, coal, mining, and agriculture, which not only export but benefit from being inflation hedges.

The outlook for the U.S. stock market has never looked grimmer, as deepening recession accompanied by higher interest rates and rising raw material costs depresses corporate earnings, and high inflation eats away at the purchasing power of people lucky enough to have jobs. That is not to say, however, that all stocks will tank or that those that do will never rebound. It stands to reason that different stocks will react in different ways to the ills about to beset us, and some will actually benefit. A look back at past hard times will show that to be true and help us to decide which stocks to hold and which to sell.

Before doing so, though, any reference to hard economic times must deal with the role played by gold, the ultimate haven. I discuss gold in detail in Chapter 6, but in the context of this discussion, the stocks of gold mining companies have special relevance. In 1933, President Roosevelt issued an order confiscating gold bullion, but that order did not extend to private ownership of shares in gold mining companies. During the devastating bear market of the 1930s, gold stocks, which leverage gold prices (as I explain in Chapter 6), soared. Homestake Mining, which operated the largest gold mine in North America (the Homestake mine itself was closed in 2002, the same year the company was acquired by Barrick Gold Corporation of Canada), had a compound annual rate of return, excluding dividends, of 35 percent between 1929 and 1935. In the 1973–1974 bear market, stocks lost

50 percent of their value, but gold mining stocks nearly quadrupled.

Historical Parallels

Stocks are widely believed to provide inflation protection, since factories, equipment, and inventories rise in value as prices generally increase. Historically, stocks have in fact tended to rise with inflation rates, but too much inflation has caused volatility and raised a question as to whether stocks really are a reliable inflation hedge.

Stocks in certain sectors have similarly earned a reputation as recession protection. Stocks designated as *defensive* are those in industries that make stuff we've simply got to have, such as food and drugs, or items in the category of *sin*, referring to things we may not need but will kill to get—traditionally tobacco and alcohol, and perhaps other things to newer generations.

Such rules of thumb are based on common sense and will always be valid, although whether they result in gains, simply lower losses, or neither, depends on the severity of the recession, the urgency of the demand, and a lot of other factors that change as a downturn proceeds.

Of course, we are not talking here about mild inflation or a minor recession except as early or late stages of the main event. The situation we are facing is of a magnitude comparable to the Great Depression of the 1930s and the next worst bear market, the stagflation period of the 1970s. There are parallels in both cases, but also ways in which the current crisis differs significantly.

In any event, the investment experience of the 1980s and 1990s, which is the only experience many readers have and which they remember as a time of prosperity and optimism, was poor preparation for what's ahead. No longer can we count on falling interest rates, decelerating inflation, and rising asset prices.

The situation we are facing is of a magnitude comparable to the Great Depression of the 1930s and the next worst bear market, the stagflation period of the 1970s.

So let's see what we can learn from the times that put stocks to the extreme test.

The 1930s

There is a very real possibility that the current recession will deepen into a repeat of the Great Depression of the 1930s, only with consumer prices rising, not falling.

In the 1930s, the problem was not inflation, but deflation. Cash grew in value as did bonds held to maturity. Stocks went both down and up and ended the decade down. Stocks that bucked the downtrends were generally the defensive and countercyclical issues. But hedging inflation was not a factor.

Speaking, though, of inflation, one of my researchers picked something up that I thought was interesting. In his book, *Winning on Wall Street* (New York: Warner Books, 1986), money manager Martin Zweig made this comment about the pre-crash 1920s:

> On a long-term basis [he is referring to the "Deflated Dow Jones Industrials," a Ned Davis Research chart plotting monthly DJIA figures adjusted for inflation] there was a tremendous bull market from 1921 to the peak in 1929. This was probably the greatest bull market in our history. Interestingly, prices were quite stable during the decade of the 1920s, with no significant inflation.

CPI figures for the period, presumably less contrived than those put out today, bear out his observation that price inflation was minimal. What Zweig finds "interesting," implying mysterious, is what I recognize, and hope you do too, as inflation showing up in rising asset prices, rather than consumer prices (which rising productivity was holding in check), as a direct consequence of the Federal Reserve's expansions of the money supply, a fact confirmed by no lesser a light than Alan Greenspan in an article written in 1966 and reprinted in Ayn Rand's *Capitalism: The Unknown Ideal* (New York: Penguin, 1987).

In 1930, every stock in the Dow Jones Industrial Average declined except three.

Anyway, the collapse that ensued bottomed out in 1930, down 89 percent from its 1929 peak, giving way to a bull market that lasted until 1937, when prices fell again until a few months after Pearl Harbor.

In 1930, every stock in the Dow Jones Industrial Average declined except three. Those that gained slightly were Liggett & Myers, General Foods, and Borden Co.— one tobacco company and two food producers. In 1931, every Dow stock was down, and the same was true in 1937. In 1933, 1935, 1936, and 1938, 80 to 90 percent of the Dow stocks showed gains.

Of course, the fortunes lost in the stock market of the 1930s were lost because so much stock was bought on margin, meaning that when prices tumbled margin calls meant putting up more money. Holding for prices to come back was not an option for many people, and those who did hold waited until the 1950s for the Dow to recover.

But the 1930s proved that food and tobacco, traditional defensive stocks, bucked the trend during the worst stock market crash in history. Gold mining shares, of course, were in a stratosphere of their own.

~

It also proved that markets don't like extreme deflation any more than they like extreme inflation.

It also proved that markets don't like extreme deflation any more than they like extreme inflation. As I stated, though, deflation (at least as it leads to falling consumer prices)—which is getting increasing publicity as a present threat—is one "problem" we won't be facing this time. Sure, as the credit bubble deflates, asset prices will fall relative to goods prices, but the Fed stands ready to replenish the money lost with freshly printed bills. However, this new money will not reinflate the busted asset bubbles, but simply drive goods prices even higher. One fact few seem to appreciate is that falling consumer goods prices were one of the few bright spots of the Great Depression, as a lower cost of living eased the pain of the economic downturn. Unfortunately, few will experience such good fortune this time around. It's yet another example of doublespeak that the government has managed to convince the public that something inherently beneficial, falling consumer prices, is actually a scourge from which it must protect us. Conveniently, the government has the perfect weapon, a printing press, which it is only too eager to use.

Of course we will see, and are already seeing, instances where prices are declining. One example I noticed recently was a health club that was lowering prices to attract membership lost because of high gas prices and general inflation. It is also possible that other services might get cheaper, such as haircuts, movie tickets, theme parks, manicures, and college tuitions, as most of these services are not exportable. Of course, some service providers will receive a boost from an influx of wealthy tourists, such as lift tickets in Aspen, which will tend to support higher prices. As Americans lose access to their credit cards, have no home equity to tap, and are forced to pay more for basic necessities, including higher taxes, insurance premiums, and interest rates, discretionary spending will collapse, causing those providing most discretionary services either to cut prices or to scale back on capacity to regain profitability on lower volume.

But inflation is now so pervasive that despite any trade-offs, the net effect will have to be rising prices. Absent hyperinflation, some prices will fall here and there but on the whole they will rise sharply—unless, of course, we measure prices in gold, in which case they will fall through the floor. However, the important concept to grasp is that asset prices will fall much further in terms of gold than will goods prices. Thus, on a relative basis, the value of what Americans own will decline relative to the cost of living. In terms of paper dollars, of course, with extreme inflation both goods and asset prices will rise, with price increases of the former far outpacing the increases of the latter. The next effect will be to render Americans much poorer, despite the nominal rise in the value of their assets.

The 1970s

Very much like present times, the 1970s combined stagnation and inflation, notably in skyrocketing gas prices, giving rise to the term *stagflation*. What was different about the 1970s, though, is that government and consumer debt was relatively moderate, with both government and mortgage debt locked in over long time periods. This gave the Fed the option of countering inflation with aggressive rate hikes when it reached double digits. Today, it doesn't have the option of raising rates significantly without triggering consumer debt defaults and mortgage foreclosures that would bring the economy to its knees.

Also, back then any new government borrowing was financed internally. Interest paid by the government was offset by interest earned by American savers. The net effect was not a net drain on national income, though there were certainly social effects of a domestic transfer of purchasing power from the less to the more affluent.

~

American taxpayers have been committed to the mother of all adjustable rate mortgages!

Now, however, approximately half our current national debt in public hands is held abroad, and an even larger share of new issues is sold abroad. As a result, significantly higher interest rates would result in meaningful drains on our national income. Furthermore, as the outstanding debt is now very short-term, higher rates will affect the total of what the government owes, not merely new borrowing. In other words, American taxpayers have been committed to the mother of all adjustable rate mortgages!

While the 1960s, called then the "Soaring '60s," will be remembered for its go-go mutual funds, its conglomerates, and concept stocks—like Four Seasons Nursing Centers of America (bankrupt by 1970) and Performance Systems, a franchiser of fast-food fried chicken restaurants, all of which came to grief by decade's end—the 1970s became famous for the "Nifty Fifty." These were a group of high-capitalization growth companies that big mutual funds and institutional investors, by then a dominant force in the market, could buy and never worry about again. Also called *one-decision* stocks and *all-weather* stocks, these big household names by 1971 were selling at 100 times earnings (when they had earnings), despite a general market decline led by everything else.

When the bear market of 1973–1974 settled in, 27 of the Nifty Fifty dropped an average of 84 percent from their 1971–1972 highs. The Dow, which closed 1972 at 1929.02, closed 1973 at 850.86 and 1974 at 616.24 before beginning its recovery the following year. In 1973, only six of the Dow stocks rose significantly, and in 1974 only five—and, with one exception, they were different stocks.

But here's what's interesting: All six of the 1973 gainers were basic/raw materials companies, consistent with a pattern discussed in detail in Chapter 5 whereby commodities and financial markets go in opposite directions. Not only that, but their returns were strong, led by Allied Chemical's total return of 73.4 percent, Alcoa's 40.6 percent, and Bethlehem Steel's 18 percent.

In 1974, stagflation had begun, with unemployment over 7 percent and inflation over 10 percent. The Arab oil embargo was in full swing, causing fuel shortages and plant closings. Two companies benefiting from the oil crisis led the Dow in 1974: Johns-Manville, which sold fuel-saving insulation materials, and United Aircraft, whose fuel-efficient jet engines were in demand from the aircraft industry.

In 1975, the market picked up again, this time led by cyclical stocks. Profiting from what was termed "a new era of pricing power," the basic industries like steel, chemicals, aluminum, paper, and copper enjoyed a short-lived revival.

By the end of the 1970s, the cyclicals were back in a slump and leaders were the energy issues and related technology stocks, small biotech issues, and defense/aerospace stocks, reacting to the Iran hostage crisis and anticipating a Republican administration. On another tier, small capitalization stocks did prove their worth as an inflation hedge, outperforming inflation and registering a positive return over the decade. In a global economy where the action is abroad, however, it is hard to imagine that small caps, which would generally have minimal, if any, international exposure, would outperform in today's market.

With that exception, the 1970s proved that in extreme inflation, stocks in general do not hold up as well as an inflation hedge. Gold, of course, is in its own world; gold mining stocks were off the charts.

The 1970s experience proved something else of great and relevant importance: The inverse market relationship of commodities (including basic materials, agriculture, energy, and metals) to stocks in general gains validity the more serious economic problems become. It's financial paper versus tangible stuff. And there's no better example than the present, as the next chapter discusses in detail.

Finally, a discussion of the relative merits of American investments and investments made abroad would be incomplete without mentioning something else that has changed. Historically, one of the prime concerns reducing the appeal of foreign investments has been the perception of greater political risks abroad. I'm thinking here of fears that foreign nations will not respect private property, or that foreign governments might nationalize businesses or be overthrown by revolutions that could lead to changes affecting overseas investors adversely.

Although the foreign markets I recommend investing in are carefully screened to minimize such risks, the fact is that today they exist in greater degree here in the United States than in developed foreign countries. As we teeter on the edge of a substantial economic collapse, our government is more likely than others to institute tax and regulatory changes detrimental to property rights and corporate profits—things like windfall profit taxes on oil companies, for example. There is probably enough respect for our Constitution to preclude outright nationalization of industry, but one wonders if confiscating profits under the pretext of an excess profit tax isn't almost as bad.

Parting Words

My basic recommendation is to restructure your domestic stock portfolio with conservative, dividend-paying, foreign stocks that will produce currency appreciation and keep you out of the collapsing dollar and immune from any desperation measures or political gambits that the United States government might resort to as the economic predicament worsens.

Some domestic stocks are worth holding onto, such as mining companies and producers of basic materials, energy, and agricultural commodities that trade worldwide in dollars and will benefit from the commodity boom discussed later. I would hold the major oil producers, but be prepared for an excess profits tax. A better bet would probably be oil service companies, which benefit more directly from a strong oil market and are unlikely to be hit with excess profits taxes. Makers of farm equipment or fertilizer companies have a proven record as a way of participating in the agricultural boom. Exporters and multinationals with good foreign exposure should also do well.

The most important part of any U.S. allocation would be to avoid like the plague any stocks largely dependent on American consumers, especially when

(continued)

it comes to discretionary purchases or repaying their debts. That would include financials, retailers, home-builders, and consumer discretionary. I would also avoid any high multiple stocks, which would exclude most technology or biotechnology companies.

Another thought: Any U.S. company not adversely affected by inflation and producing a good global earnings stream is a possible target for acquisition by a sovereign wealth fund—or private foreign buyer; bad news for the American economy but potentially good news for some American share-holders. Witness Budweiser.

Chapter Five

Hot Stuff

~

*Investing in the Commodities
Bull Market*

IF I WOKE UP to news that it had all been a bad dream and the United States economy was in the pink of health, I would still put a portion of my portfolio in basic materials, the commodities group comprising natural resources, raw materials, and agriculture. (Gold and silver are part of the group but are covered in the next chapter.) Even after the early months of 2008 saw record highs in crude oil, metals, and grains followed by a significant pullback, I am unshaken in my belief that we are still in the early stages of a secular commodity bull market that will last at least another decade. Commodities have always been a good hedge against inflation. Today they are especially attractive because the upward trend in prices, which is rooted in supply-demand imbalances, is also being fueled by central banks around the world following the Fed's lead and debasing their own currencies.

In my view, a portfolio lacking diversification in commodities is missing a critical element.

By Way of Background

Historically, commodities and financial market cycles have gone in opposite directions—when the stocks and bonds are down, commodities are up, and vice versa. The last century saw four commodities secular bull markets averaging 17 years in duration. The most recent bear market in commodities was between 1982 and 2002, coinciding with the record bull market in stocks. The so-called New Economy sucked up capital as never before to pay for fiber-optic cabling and other technology, while commodities production was almost totally neglected. When the "irrationally exuberant" stock market ran out of greater fools and finally broke in 2001, investors, acting characteristically, began shifting from paper to stuff—from claims to wealth, like stocks, which can become worthless, to physical things like commodities, which are always worth something.

——————————— ∿ ———————————

Low commodity prices cause overutilization of resources and underinvestment in capacity, resulting in low supply relative to demand—and, I should add, in opportunity for investors.

———————————————————————————

Commodities are bounties of nature, so when we talk about supply in the raw material sector, we mean the capacity of producers to convert natural resources into a form usable in industrial production. That process involves all the stages between exploration and final delivery. Since it requires real estate, management, scientific expertise, labor, equipment, and infrastructure, producers need time and investment capital to restore the capacity that got used up when the economy was booming. The boom started because cheap raw materials fattened corporate profits, which in turn attracted investment capital at the expense of the raw materials suppliers, and it ended when raw material producers faced shortages and were forced to seek renewed investment in capacity. A vicious cycle, but you can see why it took 20 years to play out and why the current bull market will be around for a while. Summarized in the stilted language of economics, low commodity prices cause overutilization of resources and underinvestment in capacity, resulting in low supply relative to demand—and, I should add, in opportunity for investors.

At no time in history were these opposing forces more in play than during the 20-year period up to 2002. The new millennium kicked off with worldwide supplies badly depleted and the stage set for a commodities rebound.

No matter how strong long-term price trends in commodities may be, it is inevitable that they will be interrupted by frequent pullbacks and rallies. Those mean opportunities for experienced traders who see the larger picture, but they can be traps for unwary investors who don't. Volatility simply comes with the territory, caused by natural catastrophes, wars, political rumors and events, hedge funds covering short positions, speculative trading in general, and a million other factors.

Forces of Nature

The secular bull market for commodities that I believe is now under way will have all the dynamics just cited, but in one critical way it will be different. Unlike previous bull markets, this one will be driven by a global development of epochal magnitude: the industrial revolutions taking place in China and India. With a combined population of 2.4 billion people, these nations are on the verge of joining the community of developed economic powers and they have newfound wealth that, once unleashed, will cause demand for commodities to reach stratospheric levels. Though these nations will unquestionably also increase their production of commodities, which means greater supply, and ultimately lower prices in their own currencies, the dollar price of these commodities will soar, as fewer yuan and rupees are saved in U.S. dollars and more are spent on actual stuff.

Nor will the United States's declining consumption be a serious drag on world demand for raw materials. Unlike Asia, the United States is a mature society industrially. Its durable goods market is replacement rather than expansion oriented, and the goods it consumes, such as cell phones, cameras, and gadgets, are less resource intensive. In addition, as a falling dollar prices more United States residents out of the market, strengthening currencies will continue to price more of the developing world into it.

With commodities, then, we get an investment twofer in the nick of time: a time-honored inflation hedge and a super bull market.

Regarding the supply/demand situation, West Africa and the former Soviet republics on the Caspian sea such as Kazakhstan and its neighbors, have huge reserves of oil and other resources that could significantly increase supply, but won't anytime soon. Political and financial obstacles exist that virtually guarantee these supplies will not find their way into the marketplace in the foreseeable future and threaten the bull market in commodities. Likewise, any belated efforts to increase drilling here in the United States, even if successful, will not bear fruit for another five to ten years, and by then any additional supply will likely be absorbed by greater demand.

With commodities, then, we get an investment twofer in the nick of time: a time-honored inflation hedge and a super bull market.

So What Commodities Are We Talking About and What Are the Ways to Play Them?

The web site of the Commodity Research Bureau (CRB), the world's leading commodities futures research, data, and analysis firm (www.crbtrader.com/), lists over 100 commodities, but the most frequently traded are those comprising the several published commodities indexes.

The Reuters/Jeffries-CRB Futures Price Index tracks 17 that are the most heavily traded. The popular Dow Jones-AIG Commodity Index lists 19 commodities. Weighted in different ways, these and the several other commodities indexes you see in newspapers all select their components from the same basic commodity sectors.

Sectors and subsectors of the Reuters/Jeffries-CRB index are representative: energy (crude oil, heating oil, natural gas); precious metals (gold, platinum, silver); grains and oilseeds (corn, soybeans, wheat); livestock (live cattle, lean hogs); industrials (copper, cotton); softs (cocoa, coffee, orange juice, sugar).

Trading futures is potentially the most profitable way to participate in a commodities bull market.

Depending on your means, your financial sophistication, your investment objectives, and your tolerance for risk, there are six principal ways to play commodities. (I exclude options on futures, which are simply too speculative).

Direct Ownership through Futures Contracts (for Advanced Investors)

1. Nondiscretionary individual account
2. Managed (discretionary) account
3. Commodity pools

Indirect Ownership (for Average Investors)

4. Index funds
5. Stocks of producing corporations or companies providing related services in resource-rich countries
6. Dividend-paying stocks of other corporations in resource-rich countries

Trading futures, which are contracts to buy or sell a particular commodity at a price set now for delivery at a future time, is potentially the most profitable way to participate in a commodities bull market because you get the full benefit of price increases, net of transaction costs and what is called *contango*, the term for carrying costs such as storage, insurance, and financing. Most contracts expire in less than two years, but delivery of the commodity rarely occurs. Instead, contracts are *rolled over*, meaning they are closed out (or *unwound*) before their expiration and are replaced with new contracts.

Contract sizes and unit prices vary widely from commodity to commodity. For example, on the Chicago Board of Trade, soybean oil contracts are for 60,000 pounds (about $35,000 per contract at today's quote) while on the New York Board of Trade (NYBOT), a contract for orange juice is 15,000 pounds (about $25,000 per contract). With a 5 percent margin requirement (a deposit, in effect, that can be as low as 2 percent or, in the case of a fully collateralized account, as high as the contract price), you could have a soybean oil contract with $1,750 down and orange juice with $1,250 down.

To appreciate what that leverage could mean, imagine a small tornado cut a path through the Florida orange groves, causing orange juice futures to rise 10 percent. Your contract is then worth $27,500 and you could sell it for a $2,500 profit. Having put down just $1,250, you have tripled your investment on a 10 percent rise in the commodity price. Considering that wheat, just to pull a handy example out of the air, has risen 150 percent in the 52 weeks preceding this writing, you get an idea of how profitable commodities can be. That's if you're a positive thinker. With your luck, maybe instead of the tornado, it rained Florida oranges and the price of the futures went down 10 percent. In that case, your $25,000 contract would be worth $22,500 and you'd lose your deposit plus $1,250, a 200 percent loss on a 10 percent drop in the commodity price. For simplicity's sake, I ignored transaction costs in this example, but they would be included in real life.

So that's show business, commodity style, and the way it actually works is that every day your account is marked-to-market. The $25,000 orange juice contract in my example would be marked up or down to reflect the price change that day, and if there was a loss, the broker would adjust your $1,250 deposit. If losses exceeded 50 percent of your deposit, you'd get a margin call telling you to come in with more money.

A bit of good news is that profits on futures trading, net of transaction costs and contango (storage, insurance, financial carrying costs), are taxed as long-term capital gains up to 60 percent and as ordinary income on the other 40 percent. At rates prevailing in 2008, you'd be looking at a blended rate of 23 percent.

Contracts held to expiration result in actual delivery (I'll spare you the usual joke about hog bellies being dumped on your front lawn), and I already explained the roll-over option. I should mention here that the roll-over process can be a little complicated. As a contract gets closer to expiration, there are fewer buyers, so experienced traders have ways of determining the optimum time to roll. Just another wrinkle that makes futures trading tricky.

Another point that's very important: The exchanges, to control volatility, have daily trading limits on respective commodities, which can make it impossible to get out of a position when the commodity is *lock limit*. That can result in losses.

Every futures contract, being a type of derivative since its value depends on the underlying asset, is subject to counterparty risk. For every buyer there is a seller, and the obligations of each are assumed by a clearinghouse, which has the function of settling trades. The clearinghouse protects itself by having margin requirements, which its clients, the commodity exchanges, pass on to the contract holders in the form of the margins we've been talking about. It hasn't happened yet to my knowledge, but it is possible that the other side of the trade, the counterparty, which is the clearinghouse (in at least one case the clearinghouse is a division of an exchange), could go bankrupt as a result of some market aberration, causing defaults. This is precisely what the government meant when it claimed that Bear Stearns was "too interconnected to fail," the connection being all the contracts to which Bear was a counterparty.

———————————— ❧ ————————————

Successful investing in commodities futures requires knowledgeable research and constant attention.

And finally, while commodities as an asset class may be in an upward trend, individual commodities have their own supply-and-demand relationships and considerations. Some are better bets than others. That's why I say successful investing in commodities futures requires knowledgeable research and constant attention.

Commodities futures, in skilled hands, can pay off handsomely. In his highly readable and informative 2007 book, *Hot Commodities*, Jim Rogers, one of the investment world's iconic figures, cites a study done at Yale, titled "Facts and Fantasies about Commodity Futures," which found that from 1962 to 2003, "the cumulative performance of futures has been triple the cumulative performance of matching equities" (meaning stocks of companies that produce commodities). I suspect that statistic, while factual, may contain an element of fantasy in that there would be a considerable difference between the cumulative performance of futures and the cumulative performance of *individuals managing futures.*

So futures are not for everybody. They do not produce income; they require extensive research and attention; they sometimes involves high order minimums and financial suitability requirements; and, if contracts are leveraged using the liberal margin rules of commodity exchanges, there is the risk of substantial loss should the market turn adversely, which it undoubtedly will from time to time.

Ways to Own Futures Contracts

As I indicated on page 91, there are six basic ways to play commodities, four of which involved ownership of futures contracts. Depending on how advanced you are, the four choices are:

1. A nondiscretionary individual account
2. A managed account
3. Commodity pool
4. Commodity index funds

Nondiscretionary Individual Account

A nondiscretionary individual account, called simply an *individual account,* opened directly with a registered futures commission merchant (FCM) or indirectly by referral from an introducing broker, puts all the decision making in your hands. I explained earlier how contracts differ from commodity to commodity and how margins work. Contango (carrying costs) also varies with the commodity. A contract for 100 ounces of gold with a value of $100,000 would weigh 6.25 pounds and obviously cost less to store than, say, a contract for 25 metric tons of lead, the value of which, $68,000, would cost less to insure. There's a lot you have to know.

Managed Account

A managed account, also called a *discretionary individual account,* is an individual account for which you give an account manager the discretion to make decisions for you. This arrangement relieves you of burdensome research and management, but it means that confidence in the manager is everything. He will be managing other accounts for other people and, while there is no commingling, you are responsible for losses in your account. You have to be sure the manager's decisions are consistent with your objectives. Since trading futures is a risky business no matter who is doing it, and you are adding fees to the carrying costs already involved with futures (while earning no income), your decision again is whether you want to go the futures route or participate in another way.

Commodity Pool

A commodity pool is yet another way of playing the commodities market directly, but here you are typically a limited partner in a pool of accounts managed as one. A commodity pool operator structures the fund and oversees transactions made by the pool's traders on the exchange floor. The advantages of pools are (1) greater diversification than you would have with an individual account, and (2) as a limited partner (you should be sure to confirm that the pool is organized as a limited partnership) you have limited liability, meaning you stand to lose no more than what you put in.

Experienced traders can make fortunes, and maybe you can too. But for average investors, there are safer ways to play commodities.

My general comment on commodity futures trading as a way to profit from the commodities bull market is that it is analogous to playing a bull stock market by day trading. It is a complicated process. Experienced traders can make fortunes, and maybe you can too. But for average investors, there are safer ways to play commodities.

Commodity Index Funds

Commodity index funds exist abundantly in the form of exchange-traded funds (ETFs) or exchange-traded notes (ETNs) and are a sensible, low-cost way to invest passively in the commodities sector and many of its subsectors representing specific commodities.

ETFs are exchange-traded mutual funds that instead of being actively managed, hold securities, in this case futures contracts, that replicate the composition of broad market indexes, such as the Reuters/Jefferies CRB Futures Price Index (RJ/CRB), and the Dow Jones-AIG Commodity Index (DJ-AIGCI). Also, iShares of Barclay's Global Investors tracks a number of particular commodities.

Traded like stocks, ETFs seek to achieve the same total return as the futures composing the index. The tracking risk, the degree to which they fall short, is generally small and is the responsibility of the fund sponsor. Unlike the total return of a stock (price change plus dividends), the total return of the ETF is made up of interest earned on the margin accounts. Since index portfolios are nonleveraged (fully collateralized), this means the total contract value, typically collateralized using short-term Treasuries; changes in the commodity prices; and the *roll yield*, which is the difference between the contract and spot prices (meaning contango or its opposite, *backwardation*, the term used when demand causes the spot price to be higher than the contract price).

Since ETF portfolios are not actively managed, the expense ratio is typically low and is composed of operating expenses for which the sponsor is held responsible. Taxes are payable at year-end as if each contract was liquidated on the last business day. Profits in open futures positions are thus taxed annually at the rates applicable to futures. Capital gains or losses and interest income on the portfolio's collateral securities are treated at the rates normally applicable to such holdings.

By far, the greatest variety of commodity ETFs, with specific baskets tailored to a variety of themes, are available on the London stock exchange. Some of my favorites include the various agricultural baskets. Investors having difficulties trading on foreign exchanges, or in tailoring specific ETFs to complement their overall portfolios, should contact Euro Pacific Capital, where we routinely handle such transactions.

Exchange-traded notes, an invention of Barclay's Global Investors, quack and waddle like ETFs but they are taxed differently and there is a question of credit risk. Exchange-traded notes have no underlying portfolio. They are senior unsecured debt instruments issued by Barclay's that promise to repay the amount of your investment plus or minus the return of the indexes they track, net of management fees of under 1 percent. Unlike ETFs, there is no tracking risk.

As for taxes, whereas ETFs make distributions taxable partly as futures and partly as whatever rates apply to their collateral investment, ETNs lump interest and capital gains adjusted for index performance into the fund's total return, which is taxable only when the ETN is closed out or matures, which could be 30 years out.

The credit risk is the small possibility of the issuer failing to honor its payback promises.

Both ETFs and ETNs track long-only indexes; there is no short-selling.

Investing

High-yielding equities of foreign companies engaged as producers of basic materials, or as providers of services to such producers, is the alternative most consistent with my investment philosophy, which is that you can get high returns and meet both long- and short-term investment objectives using a conservative investment strategy. The secret is buying a combination of value and high dividends in developed foreign economies enjoying strong growth. Investors seeking income can easily repatriate their foreign currency dividends back into dollars, usually with a currency gain. Investors seeking growth of capital can watch dividends both grow and compound. Capital appreciation is not a fundamental objective but usually happens, particularly when companies are bought at favorable prices.

With wealth shifting abroad and the United States dollar declining, returns are more often than not augmented by profits on currency conversion.

~

The secret is buying a combination of value and high dividends in developed foreign economies enjoying strong growth.

The problem with producing companies, assuming they are in developed countries with attractive economies (resource-rich countries are discussed in Chapter 8) is, first of all, finding them. Canada has its royalty trusts, of course, but producers don't exist as pure plays (where activities are restricted to one product) in all the commodities that might be attractive. Where they do exist, such as with the vertically integrated oil majors, because of their complexity it can't be taken for granted that their stock prices will directly track the prices of the commodities they produce. Remember that, in general, stock prices decline when commodity prices rise, so the stock of a commodity producer has to buck the market trend, for starters. A company might also be badly managed.

Generally, however, the correlation between commodity prices and the stock prices of the companies that produce them is positive. It is also true that the stocks of companies in a supporting role to the producer benefit as well, sometimes even more. For example, in the oil business, where behemoths like ExxonMobil dominate the industry, rising basic commodity prices—crude oil, in this example—do not register at the stock price level as fast as they do in the companies that provide supporting services. When, for example, the oil industry decides it is time to rebuild capacity, it has to invest in exploration, size up land, set up rigs, pump the oil, transport it, refine it, and sell it—all this and more before it sees a profit.

Contrast this with the experience of an oil service and drilling company such as Baker Hughes, Schlumberger, or Halliburton, which is on the scene when the exploration phase starts and making profits from the get-go. Similarly, the smart money might gravitate to the manufacturers of tractors and farm machinery when agriculture is the commodity sector and growing time an issue.

I have the benefit of my firm's research team, of course, but the Internet is also a good source of information on foreign companies and the activities they are engaged in. If you are a do-it-yourself type rather than somebody who would seek out a broker specializing in foreign stocks, my recommendation would be to select the country first (Chapters 8 and 9 will help you with that), and then identify particular companies that produce the commodities you're interested in. The final step is security analysis, and professional research is widely available.

                                                   ~

I would recommend high-dividend-paying stocks of companies engaged in commercial real estate, utilities, or other income-producing activities in countries that are resource-rich and have developed, growing economies.

If you are unable to identify companies engaged in basic materials production, I would recommend high-dividend-paying stocks of companies engaged in commercial real estate, utilities, or other income-producing activities in countries that are resource-rich and have developed, growing economies. Economic growth related to booming commodity prices will spill over into other areas of the economy. Appreciating currencies, additional jobs, rising incomes, and so on, all benefit other industries such as commercial real estate and utilities, where greater demand and higher utilization lead to enhanced profits.

Parting Words

What I want you to take away from this chapter is the knowledge that there is extraordinary excitement in commodities, which are inflation hedges in the early stages of a historic secular bull market. There are different ways you can participate, but I recommend foreign stocks in resource-rich developed countries, particularly those having primary or supporting roles in the production process, providing they meet your other investment criteria.

While it is also possible to find such companies here in the United States, in general, there are far greater opportunities abroad. Foreign companies can typically be purchased at lower multiples, and pay higher dividends, than their domestic counterparts. An important consideration, however, is that as the United States is in the early stages of a protracted economic decline, politicians are likely to look for scapegoats. Commodity companies, reaping huge windfall profits, will be likely candidates. Domestic producers, therefore, could face significant tax increases that foreign companies operating in much healthier economies will not. As we all know, it's not how much you earn but what you keep that is important.

Properly selected foreign stocks, whether they are resource-related or simply located in countries that have vibrant economies because they are

(continued)

resource-rich, will provide steady dividend income with significantly less volatility than mutual funds or commodities futures. Through compounding, currency profits, and growth, these carefully picked stocks will beat the funds and meet your investment objectives, be they income or capital accumulation.

One final thought: Do not believe Wall Street's cries of a commodity bubble. In the effort to discourage such alternative investments, Wall Street firms that were formerly unable to spot obvious bubbles in tech stocks and real estate now confidently assure all that the bull market they missed is in fact the newest bubble.

Chapter Six

The Ring in the Bull's Nose

~

*Making Money with Gold
and Silver*

IF GOLD WERE simply for filling teeth and making jewelry, it would be a commodity like any other and wouldn't need a separate chapter. Silver is in some ways a similar story but in other ways quite different. Let's first look at gold.

Digging for Gold

Gold is a scarce resource, and after 4,000 years of prospecting, I'm not holding my breath waiting for a replay of the California Gold Rush. Unlike other commodities, however, gold is hoarded rather than consumed. What's been mined is still out there. Supply, though, is always limited, meaning that demand is the main variable affecting the price of gold. Demand comes principally from sources having economic or investment interests in gold.

Gold's financial role is unique. Money gravitates to gold as a safe haven, a store of value when the purchasing power of currencies is threatened by inflation or economic instability. The United States has both problems in spades. Inflation is also becoming a big problem abroad. Not surprisingly, the price of gold has more than tripled since 2000. But we ain't seen nothin' yet. The current gold price reflects only a fraction of the inflation already in the worldwide monetary system. Inflation is also playing a huge role in our government's initiatives aimed at softening the effects of the mortgage meltdown, and some $40 trillion of unfunded future obligations like Social Security and Medicare assure the printing presses will be humming for some time to come.

I predict that when purchasing power erodes to the point where fear starts giving way to panic, the price of gold will acquire a *monetary premium,* an increase in price on top of what it gains as an inflation hedge, anticipating the surge in demand that would result if gold were reinstituted as money.

That will probably happen and when it does, the reason will be that fiat money failed once again, as it always has wherever and whenever it's been tried as a monetary system, rendering currencies worthless. The abandonment of the international gold standard in 1971 meant that all the world's currencies became fiat money, meaning money that is money merely because the issuing government says it is money—paper IOUs having no intrinsic value and worth only their purchasing power. It also means that governments previously restrained from printing more money than their gold reserves allowed were thereupon free to create systemic inflation by expanding money supplies at will.

***

With the dollar facing imminent collapse, and with foreign central banks printing their own currencies to buy dollars in politically motivated yet economically misguided attempts to manage its decline, people are responding by buying gold.

Especially in the past 20 years, the United States, as earlier noted, has been expanding the money supply steadily to keep consumers spending and to finance government programs that would otherwise have to be financed through politically unpopular taxes. Foreign countries, to remain competitive, have followed suit. So inflation, most of it hidden from the public, has been shrinking the purchasing power of fiat currencies here and abroad. With the dollar facing imminent collapse, and with foreign central banks printing their own currencies to buy dollars in politically motivated yet economically misguided attempts to manage its decline, people are responding by buying gold.

One more thing: Since March 2008, when gold went over $1,000 an ounce and then dropped some, I've been debating cynics who think gold is a bad bet. They point to 1979 when, amid record high inflation, gold first hit $850 an ounce, then abruptly dropped back down to about $300, and remained in a narrow trading range around the $400 level until 1999, before making a new low of about $250 that marked the end of a 20-year bear market and ushered in the bull market now fully underway. Just like in 1979, they argue, gold at $1,000 was a bubble that burst.

That argument is based on a false analogy and a misreading of what actually happened in 1979. It makes no sense at all. To make a long story short, gold spiked to a then all-time high that year when inflation reached into double digits and threatened to sink the dollar.

Fed Chairman Paul Volcker, choosing recession over a collapsed dollar, raised interest rates to double-digit levels. That brought inflation down and it was thereupon pronounced dead, setting the stage for a post recession period of sustained economic growth. Central bankers were heralded as modern-day messiahs, culminating with Queen Elizabeth II dubbing Volcker's successor, Alan Greenspan, with the title "Knight Commander of the British Empire" in 2002 and President Bush awarding Sir Alan the Congressional Medal of Freedom in 2005. With talent like that and with no inflation to worry about ever again, gold was back to filling teeth. And the Fed was back to printing money.

When inflation began causing concern again in 2000, gold soon began its upward trend, finally breaking through $1,000 per ounce. After making a new record high, this notoriously volatile commodity dropped back to the mid $800s range, which hardly looks like a burst bubble. In fact, to me this retrenchment amounts to a classic retest of a breakout, where prior resistance becomes new support. If the $850 ceiling, which held for almost 30 years, is now the floor, the stage is being set for an explosive rally.

———————— ∼ ————————

As the dollar continues to lose value and heads toward collapse, and foreign governments continue to intervene on its behalf, gold will continue to rise and at some point gain additional value as potential money.

A similar situation occurred with the Dow Jones Industrial Average, which peaked at 1,000 in 1966 and after several failed bear rallies eventually broke through that level for good in 1982. After consolidating the breakout above prior resistance, the new bull market in stocks began, with the Dow hitting a bull market peak of 11,750 in January 2000. (It has since eclipsed that milestone in nominal terms, but adjusted for inflation or priced in gold or stronger currencies, the 2000 peak remains the real high.) Gold's breakout and consolidation above $850 will likely prove just as significant an event and provide the foundation on which an explosive bull market will be built.

However, it is unlikely Ben Bernanke or any immediate successor will be knighted for slaying the inflation dragon. What do they think would happen today, with a nation in debt to its eyeballs, if interest rates went to double digits? Don't even think about it.

So don't be swayed by the naysayers. As the dollar continues to lose value and heads toward collapse, and foreign governments continue to intervene on its behalf, gold will continue to rise and at some point gain additional value as potential money. With the national debt, funded and unfunded, somewhere around $50 trillion, there's plenty of paper money to print and enough inflation ahead to keep gold busy. Expect volatility; that comes with the territory. Ultimately, I see gold going to $5,000 or higher before this bull market ends.

A Silver Lining

Although silver is in much greater supply than gold, its industrial market is larger and more diverse. Interestingly, though, significantly more silver is consumed than is being mined. The shortfall is partly offset by recycling, mainly in the photographic industry, but most of it is covered by above-ground stocks owned by central banks and other major holders that are being sold off. As a result, inventories have been steadily shrinking on a worldwide basis. Added to this is the situation that, unlike gold, a significant amount of silver production is consumed and disappears each year.

According to one report, the available stockpile of silver has declined from more than 2.5 billion ounces in 1980 to around 500 million ounces in 2007, less than is used in a single year. Silver is thus prone to supply-and-demand imbalances caused by shortages, making it an attractive commodity play independent of its monetary role.

That said, silver and gold prices have a high degree of correlation, although silver tends to be more volatile because of fluctuations in industrial versus inflation-related demand. Silver is second only to gold as a store of value, rising as the dollar falls, and although the like-lihood of its being monetized again is less than for gold, it does exist. So silver is bought by investors confident that a monetary premium will enhance the gains they already enjoy.

The ratio of gold to silver prices is closely watched by silver investors. The higher the ratio, the cheaper silver is relative to gold. Over the past century, gold's price aver-aged 47 times the price of silver. When these words were written, the ratio was 51.13, with gold at $920 and silver at $18. Silver began 2008 at $14, a year-to-date gain of 29 percent by April 2008.

~

Silver could have better upside than other precious metals, including gold, since it benefits from both the dollar's slide and the commodity sector's up-cycle and is also in short supply.

Generally, my feeling about silver is that it is in a bull market with commodities in general, but has more going for it. It could have better upside than other precious metals, including gold, since it benefits from both the dollar's slide and the commodity sector's up-cycle and is also in short supply. But given its historical variability, it could also have a greater downside risk.

The Six Ways to Play Gold and Silver

Broadly speaking, there are six ways to own gold and silver:

1. Physical ownership
2. Perth Mint
3. Exchange-traded funds and notes
4. Gold money
5. Commodity futures
6. Mining stocks

Let's take them one by one.

Physical Ownership

Physical ownership means buying bullion and storing it yourself or paying for storage in facilities existing for that purpose. *Bullion* refers to precious metals in their bulk form, which can be ingots (also called bars) cast in various sizes or coins, such as the South African Krugerrand, the Canadian Maple Leaf, the Australian Kangaroo, the American Eagle, and many others. The coins are sometimes legal tender with a nominal value, but you want them for their bullion value, which is determined by mass and purity and is usually much higher. (I exclude numismatics, collectors' coins whose value is determined by scarcity and condition. Although they may have bullion value, they are bought for their rarity value and really belong in the asset class called collectibles.)

People buy physical gold as a way of preserving wealth, avoiding risk, and maintaining liquidity rather than making their wealth grow.

People buy physical gold as a way of preserving wealth, avoiding risk, and maintaining liquidity rather than making their wealth grow. For getting rich, you'd buy gold-based investments, such as mining stocks, which I discuss later. Physical gold is more like cash. Instead of going up, your physical gold will hold its value as fiat currencies lose value. Because you see gold prices rising, you may think your wealth is increasing, when in fact it is merely being preserved. This is a hard point to grasp, but an important one. It helps to look at it this way. Take something like oil. The price of crude oil has been going through the roof in dollar terms because the producers are looking at the dollar's value and trying to preserve their own purchasing power. Priced in gold, oil has been relatively stable.

Bullion is bought through dealers who buy from national mints or gold refiners. The dealers work on a markup of the *spot* or daily cash price of the metal. Markups vary from dealer to dealer, so it is important to select a group of reputable dealers and then shop them for the best price.

As a general rule, since it is cheaper to make a large bar of gold than to fabricate a small coin, you get more bang for the buck buying big.

Most bullion dealers operate these days from web sites and ship by mail. Put the keyword "buy gold" in your Google search and you will get the names of dealers whose individual web sites will show prices and provide clues as to the dealer's reputability.

The web sites of three dealers who are established and considered reputable are www.amergold.com, www .Blanchardonline.com, and www.kitco.com. The Better Business Bureau (www.bbb.org) records customer complaints and is another way to narrow things down.

In buying gold coins, you should know that coins having the same weight may have different degrees of purity.

For example, the American Eagle is 91.67 percent pure while the Austrian Philharmonic is 99.99 percent pure. This does not mean they have more or less gold. They each have one ounce of gold, but different amounts of other metals for durability. The coins weigh more or less the same, but they all have an ounce of pure gold.

If you choose to store your gold somewhere other than with your dealer, yourself, or a bank's safe-deposit box, there are things to avoid. *Unallocated* accounts at bullion banks are only promises to give you back your gold when you request it, so there is a risk that if the bank becomes insolvent you could be in the position of an unsecured creditor. Pool accounts that are unallocated involve the same risk. Gold certificates may not even represent storage, only the promise of gold on presentation, so be careful of them.

Physical silver is owned similarly to gold with one exception, which happens to be my personal favorite: junk silver sold in bags containing $1,000 in face value of dimes, quarters, half-dollars, or silver dollars minted before 1968. They are 90 percent silver and legal tender—not that you'd spend them for their nominal value, which would be much less than their metallic value. The significance of their being legal tender is that they are somewhat safer from confiscation by Uncle Sam than bullion is.

Perth Mint

Perth Mint is owned by the government of Western Australia, which is AAA-rated, and fully guarantees all accounts, which are further insured by Lloyds of London. This 100-year-old mint is the only government-backed bullion storage facility in the world and it is represented in every United States state except Arizona by my own firm, Euro Pacific Capital.

The Perth Mint Certificate Program (PMCP) differs from certificate programs discussed earlier, because the metals remain on the premises and cannot be lent out.

Under the PMCP, investors can purchase bullion gold, silver, and platinum at the Perth Mint spot market ask price with no markup. You pay only a 2.25 percent service fee and a $50 administrative fee, so the cost of a minimum investment of $10,000 would be $10,275. Storage, which can be a significant cost of physical ownership, particularly with bulky silver, is free. Should you decide someday to take physical possession of your metal, you can instruct that it be fabricated into bars or coins of set weight, paying a small fee to cover the costs of doing so.

PMCP accounts are probably safe from the risk of confiscation since, unlike the United States in 1934, Australia has no history of prohibiting personal ownership of gold and could ill afford to disrupt an industry as vital to its economy as mining or to cause investors to lose faith in the scarcity of gold. Certificates, provided they are as safe as they are here, are more convenient than storing coins or bars at home or in a safe-deposit box. Since the PMCP is not a bank account, you don't have to disclose it, and should the United States ever again make it illegal to own gold, you would be at some advantage with your money out of the country.

As stated earlier, Perth Mint is represented by my own firm, Euro Pacific Capital, and I can personally attest to its service and reputability.

Exchange-Traded Funds and Notes

Exchange-traded funds (ETFs) and exchange-traded notes (ETNs) are relatively new to the scene but are proliferating mightily. What ETFs and ETNs have in common is that both represent indexes or sectors and trade as stocks. Like stocks, they can be traded using conditional orders; they can be sold short and owned on margin. They differ, though, in that an ETF holds an actual portfolio of securities whereas ETNs hold a senior unsecured debt instrument that promises to repay the amount of your investment adjusted by the performance of a specified index.

Exchange-traded funds replicating indexes have operating expenses and thus don't match the indexes exactly. The difference varies between funds and is called *tracking risk*.

An ETN has no portfolio and thus no tracking risk, but the investor is a creditor and thus has credit risk.

There is also a difference in the way they are taxed. Exchange-traded funds are taxed at the rates applying to the underlying securities as if they were sold at year-end. The ETN lumps interest and gains or losses on index performance into one total return figure, taxable when the ETN is closed out or matures, which could be years later.

There is a growing list of ETFs that track either gold or silver or a combination of both metals and that trade on both domestic and foreign stock and commodity exchanges. Gold ETFs, called GETFs, track the price of gold and hold certificates for physical bullion that are on deposit and insured. Silver ETFs also hold certificates instead of bullion.

The Internet has lists of GETFs and Silver ETFs, but three that come to my mind are SPDR Gold Trust (the Trust) (formerly StreetTRACKS Gold Trust, or GLD) and iShares COMEX Gold Trust (IAU), both traded on the New York Stock Exchange, and iShares Silver Trust (SLV), traded on the American Stock Exchange.

As for ETNs, Deutsche Bank announced in February 2008 that it would launch three ETNs offering short, long, and leveraged trading strategies in gold. The press release stated: "These products are the first of their kind and fill a need in the market for the investor who really follows gold and is looking for a sophisticated way to get leveraged or short exposure to it." The ETNs are DB Gold Double Short ETNs (DZZ.P), DB Gold Double Long ETNs (DGP.P), and DB Gold Short ETN (DGZ. P). All three track the DB Liquid Commodity Index–Optimum Yield Gold Index and trade on the New York Stock Exchange Arca, a division specializing in derivatives and ETNs. And there are others.

My general feeling about these exchange-traded funds is that there is always some risk that the auditing is unreliable and the metal behind the certificates is not really there. So why, unless you value the trading possibilities that go with exchange listing, take the chance when you can own the metals outright? As to the exchange-traded notes, there is credit risk at a time when the credit markets are in turmoil. Again, why risk that when you can own the physical commodity yourself?

Also, since GETFs are just as subject to confiscation as physical gold, if you decide to invest that way to have the advantages of being exchange-traded, you might feel safer with the Australian, Canadian, or British products.

I'm also slightly uncomfortable with newly introduced products that don't have a self-regulatory organization to oversee questions having to do with the liabilities and responsibilities of the custodians and other market participants, with matters concerning fees, valuations, and expenses, and with questions of purity and fair market practices generally. So invest with caution.

Gold Money

Gold money already exists in the form of *digital gold*, which is accessed using the Internet's electronic payments systems using a debit or credit card and facilitated by cyber accounting technology. You don't have to carry gold around, and transacting small or large amounts from your central bullion deposit is a matter of simple bookkeeping.

GoldMoney may be the best monetary system ever, and if governments don't adopt it, I predict it will be widely used as a commercial service.

GoldMoney.com was founded by James Turk, a highly regarded figure in gold circles whose investors and shareholders include two publicly traded gold mining companies, DRDGold Limited (South Africa) and IAMGOLD Corporation (Canada). GoldMoney's main office, web site, and database servers occupy a state-of-the-art facility on Jersey, one of the British Channel Islands in the English Channel. It operates somewhat like online banking, but your account is denominated in *goldgrams* and mils rather than dollars and cents. Each GoldMoney goldgram you buy represents ownership of your own pure gold, which is in allocated storage in a specialized bullion vault near London and is insured by Lloyd's of London.

GoldMoney conveniently and speedily handles payments in gold between members in exchange for goods and services. Transactions are processed instantly. Your gold stays in the vault, but fractional ownership of it changes as payments are made. It may be the best monetary system ever, and if governments don't adopt it, I predict it will be widely used as a commercial service.

GoldMoney also operates as a retailer of bullion aiming to making gold buying economical and practical for average individuals. Customers can buy any fraction of a gold bar at a couple of percentage points above the spot price, far less than the markup you'd pay a dealer. Check it out at www.goldmoney.com.

Commodity Futures

Commodity futures are discussed in Chapter 5 and there is little I would add in the particular case of gold and silver. You can bet the ranch by taking advantage of the liberal margin rules of the commodity exchanges and make or lose a fortune, or you can fully collateralize your account, buy a contract, and roll it over without taking any more risk than you would owning physical gold or silver outright. Or you can do something in between, putting up as much collateral and taking as much risk as you want.

As I stressed in Chapter 5, though, there is counter-party risk whenever you get into derivatives, whether you're buying a futures contract or trying to protect yourself against trading loss by using put options. If the exchange goes bankrupt—and these days nothing would surprise me—you're out of luck.

Mining Stocks

Mining stocks offer the prospect of income and capital gains magnified by leverage, and are potentially the most profitable way to play gold and silver.

Gold and silver prices rise and fall with inflation and so do the stocks of mining companies, but not in lockstep. The price of the metal has to rise faster than the cost of producing it before miners become profitable enough to attract investors, and inflation has a more direct impact on production costs than on the price of the world's greatest inflation hedge. Ironic as that is, it's an eloquent comment on the government's success in soft-pedaling the real extent of the inflation problem.

So, as this book was being written, and gold prices are making record gains, gold mining shares are lagging and most are not paying dividends. But that will change. For now, many gold miners remain the ironic victims of inflation, as the cost of mining rises faster than the price of gold. However, once investors fully appreciate the threat, the price of gold should surge, propelling the entire mining sector, silver included, into a major bull market. And in 5 or 10 years, look for a mania that makes the NASDAQ bubble seem like a warm-up.

───────────────── ∼ ─────────────────

If gold prices pan out the way I believe they have to, the mining stocks, silver included, will soon be in their own bull market. And in 5 or 10 years, look for a mania that makes the NASDAQ bubble seem like a warm-up.

───────────────────────────────────

Mining has high fixed costs, a negative when production is at low levels but a boon when times are good. And stocks provide leverage. A 10 percent increase in the price of gold could easily mean a 50 percent increase in the profits of a mining company.

The mining industry can be viewed as four parts of a risk pyramid. At the lowest and most conservative level are the major players. The largest, and the only mining stock in the Standard & Poor's 500, is Newmont Mining. It sells roughly 5 million ounces per year (at $1,000 an ounce, that's $5 billion) and has somewhere between 85 million and 100 million ounces in reserves. Others at this level include Barrick Gold Corporation, Gold Fields Ltd., AngloGold Ashanti Ltd., Harmony Gold Mining, and Goldcorp Inc.

Hedging, where miners protect themselves from falling prices by contracting to buy or sell given amounts of gold at given prices months or years in advance, thereby losing profits if prices rise, has traditionally been something analysts discount as they project earnings and stock values. In the current environment, however, hedge books have been greatly reduced. Newmont does no hedging and Barrick, one of the most notorious hedgers, had its hedge book down to 2 million ounces last year, from 8 million a few years before. In any event, proceeds from hedging, in effect borrowed money, have been invested in exploration projects that would likely result in discoveries exceeding the remaining ounces currently being hedged.

The mid-tier group is slightly less conservative but comprises producing companies that are smaller but well established and very solid. Examples are Newcrest Mining, Franco-Nevada, Agnico-Eagle Mines Ltd., Yamana, and Kinross Gold Corporation. The attraction of this group is that with most analysts focused on the majors, they can get lucky with new projects without attracting a lot of attention and publicity that would goose their stock. You can find winners here and they should be included, with the majors, in an intelligently structured portfolio.

The next level, called the juniors, consists of smaller, younger companies that have reserves and are in production.

These include Bema Gold, Northern Orion Resources, Golden Star Resources Ltd., Taseko Mines Ltd., and Northgate Minerals Corporation. What I said about the mid-tier group applies to the juniors, although the risk here is greater.

The top-tier companies are the riskiest, of course, and arguably should not be called mining companies. Sometimes called *property plays,* they do not own gold; their thing is exploration. They are the so-called penny stocks. Some of them will hit it big—most of them won't. If I could tell you which was which, I probably wouldn't be writing a book.

Silver mining is not the independent industry that gold mining is, although there are a few major silver producers, such as Hecla Mining Company (NYSE:HL) and Pan American Silver Corporation (NASDAQ:PAAS), that together with others account for about 25 percent of world production. The rest is produced as a by-product of miners specializing in copper or other metals, including gold. Agnico-Eagle Mines Limited, mentioned earlier as a mid-tier gold producer, produces silver, copper, and zinc as by-products. Cannington, a copper producer in Australia, produces silver.

Except where noted, what I have said about gold as an investment applies to silver, although silver has both greater upside potential and greater downside risk.

Parting Words

People always ask my opinion on portfolio alloca-
tions, and I can actually get pretty specific on the
subject. I recommend overall portfolios that have
a 10 to 30 percent representation in gold-related
investments. Of the gold portfolio, I suggest 20 to
50 percent be in physical gold, some in your posses-
sion and somewhat more offshore. The rest should
be in mining stocks, preferably in developed foreign
countries where valuations are better and there is
less risk of mines being nationalized or subjected
to excess profits taxes or of private holdings being
confiscated.

My recommended allocation with respect to mining stocks would be 40 percent majors, 30 percent
mid-level, 20 percent juniors, and 10 percent exploration companies and speculative stocks. Silver, if
desired, should be blended in following the same
percentage guidelines.

Fiat money everywhere is going to continue to
decline in value, and gold and silver prices will rise
in reaction as a bull market in commodities generally continues for at least another decade. Gold will
add a monetary premium to its price and ultimately
replace fiat currency, if not officially, then as pri-
vately promulgated digital money.

Chapter Seven

Weathering the Storm

~

*Following the Money
to Foreign Soil*

PARTICULARLY WITH THE DOLLAR in a swan dive, it makes obvious sense to invest in foreign countries where wealth is growing, provided the offsetting risks are reasonable. As our purchasing power is being transferred from the dollar to the currencies of nations that produce the goods we consume, we simply must invest where that purchasing power is flowing so we can preserve our wealth and make it grow. Those who fail to do so will suffer substantial declines in their standards of living as consumer price increases outpace their incomes.

Steering Clear of the Garden of Worms

Foreign investing has always come with caveats, which has made investors reluctant to follow this path. As long as we're investing in established companies in developed countries, we really don't have to worry anymore about such traditional concerns as inadequate financial reporting and accounting regulation. American auditing standards of disclosure and transparency are widely applied in the developed economies. Of course, watching former executives of companies like Enron, WorldCom, and Tyco International trade their Brioni striped suits for government-issued striped pajamas reminds us that the integrity of corporate financial statements should never be taken for granted—domestically or abroad.

Political risk, which I discussed in Chapter 4, while an important consideration in emerging economies, is actually less important in developed foreign economies than it is right here in the good old USA given the precarious state of our economy. Excess profits taxes, confiscation of gold, even the prospect of laws prohibiting foreign investment, are all examples of actions that either have precedent here or could become enactments affecting American investors. The likelihood of similarly adverse political developments in strong and growing developed economies is much more remote.

The one risk of foreign investing that exists regardless of the merits of the investment is currency exchange risk—the risk that when we convert income or sales proceeds from a foreign currency to the dollar, we will experience a loss because the dollar has become stronger. That, of course, will be the least of our worries looking ahead. While I can't promise that the dollar won't be in a bear market rally when you convert—trends are always subject to interruption—the dollar's downward trend against other major currencies will continue for as long as the United States has inflation, high debt, and trade deficits.

Another concern investors new to the foreign markets often have is the fear that foreign proceeds or dividend payments can't be readily converted to dollars you can spend here. Rest assured that the investments we talk about here will be liquid, meaning you can sell them on a phone call, and that you can immediately repatriate funds.

So foreign investing doesn't really entail any serious inconvenience. Nor does it hold any inherent risks simply because it is foreign, assuming you invest in solid companies located in countries that have minimal political or economic risks. (Emerging economies entail various risks and hold the prospect of higher returns, which is why we discuss them separately in Chapter 9.)

Fact or Fiction?

Were the entire global economy to go down the tubes, there would be little point in investing anywhere. But that's not going to happen, which brings me again to the issue of decoupling. I touched upon that in Chapter 2 to reassure readers that getting out of cash and bonds and into safe non-dollar-denominated investments was still possible thanks to economic decoupling, which meant other global economies would remain strong despite what happens here. Because the continuing negative reaction of worldwide markets to America's economic unraveling has revived what in my opinion is a rather silly debate about whether decoupling is reality or myth, I want to share some further thoughts on that critical issue before getting into the questions of how and where to invest abroad.

-------------------------- ∾ --------------------------

To conclude that the American consumer is vital to the economies that produce the goods we import ignores Asian realities and confuses the engine of economic growth with its caboose.

Since we do, after all, represent nearly 30 percent of the world's gross domestic product, it would be unreasonable to expect foreign countries in a global economy to be impervious to major upheavals here. Impervious, though, isn't the point. The important thing is that the fundamentals of economies abroad be solidly in place so that adjustments and adaptations made necessary by America's problems can proceed with minimal disruption.

That's what decoupling is about, and it is a concept with two sides, economic and financial, which exist separately but are both in very favorable trends.

Repeating what I said in Chapter 2, from the economic standpoint, to conclude that the American consumer is vital to the economies that produce the goods we import ignores European and Asian realities and confuses the engine of global economic growth with its caboose.

Sure, the dollar's collapse will cause short-term disruptions in the economies of Asia and, to a lesser extent, Europe. But unburdened with debt, and with trade accounts generally in surplus, these producing economies—which are the *real* engines of growth—are in much stronger shape fundamentally than we are. They will be stronger still when they finally become their own best consumers. So economic decoupling is already happening and will be picking up its pace rapidly.

Financial decoupling has to do with global stock markets being synchronized with one another. That will follow economic decoupling, but there is no question that it will happen. Japan's stock market was in the doldrums for a decade in the 1990s, but the only investors who really got hurt were those who remained invested there. People who invested ex-Japan made out fine. Also, I suspect the credit crunch being felt abroad and affecting foreign stock markets is largely the result of losses on loans to American borrowers. But Americans won't be borrowing as much from abroad in the future, so the global credit crunch there will soon be over—replaced, I'll bet, by another savings glut. So it will take a little time for financial decoupling to catch up with economic decoupling. In the meantime, the pullback being experienced in foreign stocks is an opportunity for Americans to buy at favorable prices.

The Asian economies that have borne the brunt of the cost of subsidizing American consumption, a cost paid in lower standards of living, will be the most affected initially by the loss of American consumption, but also the ones poised for the most dynamic growth, as they enjoy a more efficient allocation of resources and begin satisfying their own appetites for consumption. It will be the American caboose, in effect, that gets decoupled from the global gravy train. Unencumbered by all that dead weight, the real engine of economic growth will burn up the tracks.

And don't think this can't happen in the short term. I see it as analogous to the American experience during and immediately after World War II. An economy totally converted to wartime production was able, almost overnight, to revert to peacetime production and create unprecedented economic growth. There's no reason a similarly rapid transition can't take place in Asia.

Rather than worry about foreign economies, let's invest in them.

Investing in Foreign Economies

In this chapter, I want to show you the financial basics of investing in foreign stocks (specific regions and countries representing the best investment opportunities are discussed in Chapters 8 and 9). As mentioned earlier, I strongly prefer conservative, dividend-paying foreign stocks to foreign bonds, because inflation prevails in all countries using fiat money and stocks offer inflation protection. So I'll be talking about stocks, although they can be owned in different ways.

I strongly prefer conservative, dividend-paying foreign stocks to foreign bonds, because inflation prevails in all countries using fiat money and stocks offer inflation protection.

The paths of least resistance to folks new to foreign investing may not be the best ones, so let's look first at American Depositary Receipts, mutual funds, exchange-traded funds, and other investment vehicles that are alternatives to buying individual stocks on foreign exchanges.

American Depositary Receipts

American Depositary Receipts (ADRs) were designed to make investing in foreign stocks easier for Americans. They are receipts for the foreign shares that are held in domestic bank vaults, are listed on United States stock exchanges, and entitle their owners to dividends, reports, voting privileges, and other shareholder rights.

While they succeed in accomplishing their purpose, I have a few problems with them. The first and probably the most important one is that they are issued by the biggest and most visible foreign corporations, names like Sony and Toyota, which is both good news and bad news. Obviously companies of such stature are solid investments paying reliable dividends. But, like blue chips generally, they are normally *fully priced*, as we say in the business, meaning that if you want undervalued stocks with higher yields, you're better off investing directly on foreign exchanges. In addition, as they earn substantial percentages of their profits in the American market, their earnings in the short run will be negatively affected by a weakening U.S. dollar and the collapse of our consumer-driven economy.

Also, banks incur costs in issuing ADRs, and they may deduct from dividends to reimburse themselves. Another factor is that ADRs are subject to the same onerous and costly regulations as American companies; many well-run foreign companies, therefore, choose not to sponsor them.

All this said, ADRs do offer convenience, so it's up to you to decide if you want that more than value and yield.

Mutual Funds

Mutual funds, meaning open-end funds bought and redeemed at their net asset values (NAV) and holding foreign portfolios, are widely available. They offer diversification and professional management, and charge annual management fees, which are usually less than 1 percent of NAV. Minimum purchase amounts vary from nothing to $2,500 and there are apt to be sales charges (called *load*) and other charges, depending on whether you buy the fund directly, as with Fidelity and Dreyfus, for example, or through an investment adviser.

Before working with mutual funds, be sure you understand the distinction between international funds and global funds. Global funds hold domestic stocks as well as foreign stocks, whereas international funds comprise foreign stocks exclusively. International funds differ widely in the amount of risk they undertake, so when you see a fund sporting high yields because of higher exposure to emerging countries or companies, make sure you understand the risk is greater.

Here are the problems I have with mutual funds in general.

- As they compete with one another on the basis of quarterly performance, their focus is short-term, which often means lost opportunities.
- Their general practice is to enhance return by taking greater risk and then eliminating that risk through diversification that would otherwise be unnecessary. The same or better returns can be gained just as safely by buying more conservative, dividend-paying stocks with more limited diversification.
- Companies in which these funds invest must be large enough to fit their portfolio size, ruling out smaller companies offering greater opportunity.
- Because they are restricted to high-capitalization stocks, even international funds are bound to include multinational foreign companies with significant U.S. dollar exposure and earnings vulnerable to the American economy and its consumers.

- Management expenses applied annually cause reduction in returns that wouldn't exist in a private buy-and-hold portfolio.
- Funds that hedge currency risk increase expenses and reduce returns when a primary reason for investing internationally is to gain currency profits.
- Short-term focus precludes buying value stocks, meaning stocks that are out of favor and therefore undervalued.
- Fund redemptions, which increase when owners are under financial strain, force trading, which has tax consequences that could otherwise be avoided.
- Managed funds have a tendency to overtrade to justify their fees. In so doing, they add additional costs and subject shareholders to unnecessary capital gains taxes that ultimately reduce long-term performance.

Exchange-Traded Funds

Exchange-traded funds replicating indexes, which represent foreign regions and individual countries and can be traded like stocks, are a new and interesting alternative to investing directly in foreign companies. Being unmanaged portfolios, they have low expenses (average of expenses as a percentage of assets is 0.40 percent versus 0.65 percent for open-end index funds and as high as 2 percent for open-end mutual funds).

The catch here is that you have to buy into the idea of index (or *passive*) investing, which holds that over time, indexes outperform managed portfolios. That's another way of saying that most managers fail to beat the average performances of stocks composing the universe they compete in, which has to be true because the average managed portfolio performance is what the index is measuring to begin with.

Anyway, let's not go there; it gets into efficient market hypotheses and that sort of thing. Suffice it to say that index investing assures you of average performance, net of expenses, which is fine for a lot of people. Being a money man myself, I've got to believe I can make market-beating stock selections, if that's the name of the game.

Few, if any, ETFs offer a basket of stocks that I would consider ideal given the economic environment I envision. A prospective client of mine recently objected to paying me a commission to build and purchase a diversified portfolio of foreign dividend-paying stocks when there were several ETFs that provided similar diversification but at a lower cost. However, upon closer examination, the ETFs he referenced were composed of better than 40 percent financials, leaving the funds highly exposed to a weakening U.S economy. In addition, although these ETFs were marketed as being high dividend paying, the yields were under 4 percent, while the yield on the portfolio that I had proposed was about 7 percent.

In general, here are the pros and cons of exchange-traded index funds:

Pros
- Diversification.
- Liquidity. ETFs are traded like stocks, and limit orders and other conditional orders can be used just like stock.
- Low expenses, as described earlier.
- Tax efficiency. Since there is little or no turnover, capital gains distributions are minimal.
- Flexibility. You can decide when to sell ETF shares and create capital gains.

Cons
- Tracking risk, reflecting the difference between the ETF and the index it represents, a function of operating expenses.
- Transaction costs, which are the brokerage commissions charged whenever an ETF is bought or sold.
- Because fractional shares are not traded, ETFs are impractical for investors who dollar-cost average.

Other Vehicles

Exchange-Traded Notes (ETNs)

This new breed of investment was discussed earlier in its commodity and precious metals applications, and what I said there generally applies here. Like ETFs, exchange-traded notes (ETNs) are exchange-traded funds that track foreign and domestic market indexes, but unlike ETFs, they don't hold portfolios. They are unsecured bonds that at maturity pay you the principal plus or minus the return of the index they track less a management fee of 1 percent or less. Typically, principal is not guaranteed, but when it is, there is a trade-off of some of the index gain, making the return less than that of an ETF tracking the same index. There is counterparty risk and an unresolved issue as to whether profits at maturity (no income is paid during the holding period) are ordinary income or capital gains. They are getting more complex every day, and I'd avoid them. One example: Capital Protection Notes, based on the Morgan Stanley Capital International Europe, Australasia, and Far East (EAFE) stock index. The ticker symbol is EEC.

Unit Investment Trusts (UITs)

Unit investment trusts (UITs) holding unmanaged foreign stock portfolios are another new development. They typically mature in two to three years, thus creating a capital gains liability you could avoid by investing directly, but my main objection is their cost, which typically includes a front-end load as high as 4 percent plus transaction costs. Another drawback is that since the UITs are unmanaged during their initial durations, no adjustments are possible should market conditions change. In short, UITs are basically gimmicks that are laden with excessive fees that benefit the firms that sponsor them and the brokers who sell them at the expense of investors. Stay away.

Closed-End Funds (CEFs)

These interesting investment vehicles have been compared to a water bed on a boat, where the bed and boat bounce around in response to separate dynamics. Investors own publicly traded shares in a corporation that holds a specialized portfolio of stocks (or bonds), the net asset value of which may be higher or lower per share than shares in the fund itself. These investments are so unique they can almost be considered an asset class in themselves, but they can be a profitable investment if you buy when the fund shares are selling at a discount to the portfolio value and when and if the fund price converges with the net asset value, which may happen naturally or in accordance with the terms of the fund charter. If you decide to go the CEF route, buy when the portfolio represents a discount, make sure you know what the portfolio holds (you may think you're buying foreign stocks but then learn the portfolio has a preponderance of domestic stocks), and find out under what conditions the portfolio and fund share values are reconciled (e.g., some convert to open-end mutual funds at specified dates).

The Better Option

As I explain in Chapter 8, I use a top-down approach to stock selection. This means that I decide first what regions, what countries, and what sectors represent the best economic backdrop for investment at this time.

~

A safe, high-yielding stock that is bought and held meets any investor's objectives, whether they be aggressive or more conservative, provided they understand the risks and have appropriate time horizons.

So how do you choose individual stocks? My investment strategy keeps it very simple. I am looking for safety and for good yield. My reasoning is that a safe, high-yielding stock that is bought and held meets any investor's objectives, whether they be aggressive or more conservative, provided they understand the risks and have appropriate time horizons. As I am also looking to maximize returns while minimizing transactions costs, I buy common stocks through foreign exchanges. This also gets the benefit of yields with inflation protection and enhanced by profits on currency exchange.

Companies engaged directly in the production of raw materials, particularly when they are close to the source, can be both safe and high-yielding and offer growth potential as well. But any conservative stock, such as utilities investments and real estate in the form of commercial property trusts, are among the safest and highest-yielding. They are good bets if they are located in an economy that is strong and growing because it is resource-rich.

Beware of Pink Sheets

Buying individual stocks on foreign exchanges is, for my money, the best way to go. However, it requires working either through a broker abroad, which often means multiple brokerage accounts and even face-to-face meetings, or through domestic brokers who can trade directly on foreign exchanges. Odd as it may seem, even the largest brokers sometimes decide that brokering foreign stocks on foreign exchanges doesn't make economic sense for them, which doesn't necessarily mean they'll refuse your business. What they'll often do is process your order using Pink Sheets, which are a trap waiting for foreign stock investors unaware of them.

Pink Sheets LLC is a New Jersey company that provides daily bid and offer quotes from market makers. Market makers are broker-dealers acting in their capacity as dealers, meaning principals trading for their own accounts, as opposed to agents, which is what brokers are when they represent buyers and sellers and the market is made by an exchange. Quotes are printed on pink paper for foreign stocks, yellow paper for bonds.

~

Avoid ordering foreign stocks through a brokerage firm that might be using a Pink Sheets market maker to execute them.

The fly in this ointment is that market makers work on a spread, meaning the difference between a bid and offer price. That can be wide enough to drive a truck through if a stock is thinly traded and the price is under one dollar per share, which is typical in the United Kingdom and most Asian nations, except for Japan. Most Asian markets require *board lot* minimum trades that can range from as few as 100 shares to as many as 20,000 shares. So a stock selling for the dollar equivalent of 20 cents per share with a board lot of 10,000 shares would trade in increments of $2,000.

If the Pink Sheets market maker in that example were to make a market between the 15 cent bid and 25 cent offer, and you buy on the bid and sell on the offer, the share price would have to appreciate by 50 percent for you to break even. It's the way penny stocks traded in the United States are treated, except that in this case we are not dealing with penny stocks. Therefore, the Pink Sheets market maker makes an obscene profit (that he is not required to disclose), in addition to which a discount broker will also charge the sizable commission that applies to large-quantity penny stock orders.

The moral of this story is to avoid ordering foreign stocks through a brokerage firm that might be using a Pink Sheets market maker to execute them.

How, Then, Do You Go About Selecting a Broker Who Will Execute Your Foreign Stock Orders on a Local Foreign Exchange?

As I said earlier, opening an account with a local broker in the country you are investing in is an option, but one that is impractical for many reasons, not the least of which is that you'd be repeating the exercise in every other country you'd invest in to get diversification. You'd save on commissions, but that would be the only advantage.

My own firm, of course, Euro Pacific Capital, provides these services (visit our web site at www.europac .net to find offices convenient to your location). There are a few other firms doing this as well, perhaps more by the time you read this book.

———————————— ∼ ————————————

You can open an account with Euro Pacific
Capital by telephone at 800-727-7922 or online at
my web site at www.europac.net/account.asp. My
web site is updated daily and provides news and
commentary on our unfolding economic crisis.
The site is also a source of various special reports
and my free newsletter, *The Global Investor.* I also
do a weekly live radio show, *Wall Street Unspun*,
every Wednesday at 8:00 PM EST. The show can
be heard on shortwave (5.07 megahertz) and on
my web site, www.europac.net.

A specialized broker will be a source of helpful guidance on structuring your foreign stock portfolio. Here
are five questions I would suggest you ask them:

1. What will I be charged to effect foreign exchange
   transactions?
2. How can I be assured my order will be executed
   directly on the local foreign exchange, and not by a
   market maker in the United States using the Pink
   Sheets?
3. Can I place conditional orders (such as limit orders
   that restrict execution to a specified price or better) in foreign currencies?

4. Can I elect to receive dividends as well as proceeds from sales directly in a foreign currency?
5. Are there minimum transaction amounts, special fees for overseas orders, other hidden costs, or miscellaneous fees? Please provide a list of all charges.

Parting Words

In previous chapters, I have explained why I believe commodities, natural resources, and precious metals like gold and silver are in exciting bull markets while the dollar and financial assets generally are in for a long period of painful correction. These bull markets, however, can be played with common stocks, called *ordinaries* abroad, of companies engaged in either the production of raw materials or the mining of gold and silver, thereby getting you the leverage common stocks provide; or companies, such as utilities and real estate trusts, that are integral parts of the economies that will prosper because they are resource-rich or because they are potential consumers of their own production and will benefit from the transfer of purchasing power from the United States.

Using my top-down investment strategy, more than half the battle is knowing where geographically to put money as the dollar collapses and wealth transfers. Individual stock selection is thus reduced to the simplest and most conservative basics.

(continued)

My recommendation is to maximize returns by buying common stocks through foreign exchanges, thus minimizing transaction costs, and getting the benefit of yields that have inflation protection and are enhanced by profits on currency exchange. To accomplish that, however, you will need a specialized broker. The second choice, I believe, would be to invest in exchange-traded funds that incorporate the strategies and themes I advocate, and that focus on my favorite sectors and markets. Now let's take a closer look at some of those specific countries and sectors.

Chapter Eight

Favorite Nations

~

*Money Cat Knows Where
the Money Tree Grows*

WHEN IT COMES to foreign investing, I'm a top-down kind of guy, meaning I decide first *where* I'm going to invest, then the sectors to invest in, and last *what* stock I'm going to buy. In the bottom-up approach, analysts focus on particular companies in hopes of finding hidden values that might cause a stock price to rise despite negative industry or economic conditions. This approach has an important place in investing generally, but it doesn't work well in international investing. International returns come mostly from wise country and sector selection.

So for our purposes, I make regional and country selection my first order of business, and sector selection my second. Once I've done that, I figure my stock will be a winner if it gets me a positive return from at least two of three sources: dividend income, currency exchange, and capital appreciation.

Dividend income, of course, is company-specific and always positive. While yields are generally better abroad than in the United States, keep in mind that they do range higher or lower from country to country. But with the dollar sinking against foreign currencies, your profits on currency conversion are likely to outweigh even the highest yields—depending on the value of a country's local currency relative to the United States dollar. I discuss my favorite countries later on.

Capital gain or loss is subject to the vagaries of the market, but is more often than not a small positive. That's because even though I buy and hold dividend payers rather than growth stocks, I do look for value and some appreciation normally occurs during the holding period in line with economic growth.

I must say, though, speaking of price changes, that as I write this, foreign markets are still in a state of pullback

———————— ~ ————————

**Foreign markets are still in a state of pullback
following the mortgage meltdown and credit
crisis in the United States. While short-term
pressures may persist, I think it's an
excellent buying opportunity.**

following the mortgage meltdown and credit crisis in the United States. While short-term pressures may persist, I think it's an excellent buying opportunity.

Anyway, when it gets down to stock selection, we're not looking for ten-baggers, the term for highfliers that Peter Lynch, the legendary former manager of the Magellan Fund, contributed to the argot of investing, though we have certainly had our share. We want solid non-dollar-denominated stocks that pay high dividends, which you can use for income or allow to compound, depending on your investment objectives. Either way, we preserve and enhance our wealth with less risk, so that when the U.S. economy gets back on its feet and profit opportunities begin reappearing, we'll be in a position to capitalize, unlike those who stayed in the dollar.

Enough, then, for now, about foreign stocks. What I want to get into here is how my top-down investment strategy focusing on developed foreign economies offers a winning combination of simplicity, safety, and profitability.

What makes it relatively simple is that there are a limited number of developed economies, and the ones we'll be focusing on are politically stable, are hospitable to foreign investment, have adequately efficient stock markets, and have currencies expected to appreciate against the U.S. dollar for the foreseeable future. They are countries I've been investing in and following closely for most of my 20-plus-year career in the investment business.

What separates developed economies from developing (or emerging) economies, which are a different kind of opportunity that I discuss in a separate chapter, are factors like accelerated rates of economic growth, low taxes, pro-business regulatory systems, high savings rates, comfortable standards of living, an educated populace, a latent capacity for consumption, and some workable combination of free market forces and government intervention, among others.

Stay focused on those foreign companies that derive their earnings domestically or through trade outside the United States.

As I'll explain, it's important to avoid foreign companies with significant exports to the United States. These companies will suffer slumping earnings as the U.S. recession deepens and the dollar's decline accelerates. But keep them on your radar screen: At some point they will be excellent buys, as it will take a while for most investors to realize that earnings lost in the United States will ultimately be replaced with much higher earnings in the rest of the world. In the meantime, stay focused on those foreign companies that derive their earnings domestically or through trade outside the United States.

The broad regional breakdown of developed foreign economies consists of the following: Canada; the 15 countries comprising the Eurozone and using the euro (Austria, Belgium, Cyprus, Finland, France, Germany, Greece, Ireland, Italy, Luxembourg, Malta, the Netherlands, Portugal, Slovenia, and Spain); European countries outside the Eurozone (Switzerland, the United Kingdom, Denmark, Norway, and Sweden); Asia (Hong Kong, Singapore, Japan, Taiwan, South Korea, Thailand, and the Philippines); Australia; and New Zealand.

The regional breakdown has less practical significance, in my opinion, than other groupings I'll mention in a minute. An obvious exception would be the countries comprising the European Union (or Eurozone, Euro bloc, or Euroland, as the EU is also called), which now represents the world's largest economy (based on the market value of its GDP) with a common currency (the euro) that could possibly replace the United States dollar as the world's reserve currency. The European Union, despite socialism, has made strides in overcoming what some wag called "eurosclerosis" and is showing earnings growth.

An added observation about regions is that countries in geographical proximity tend to have higher correlations in terms of market cycles.

An example of a more useful grouping would be the natural resources bloc, comprising Australia, New Zealand, Norway, and Canada. They provide geographical diversification, and together they represent an industrial sector expected to see explosive growth over the coming decade.

Another grouping that I call the producing and saving countries is made up of Hong Kong, Singapore, Japan, Taiwan, South Korea, Thailand, and the Philippines. These Pacific Rim countries have been producing what the United States has been consuming and will suffer lower sales initially as a result of reduced American consumption. At the same time, they have become robust economies with significant exports to other Asian countries and with enough potential consumer demand in their own populations to replace the American market as quickly as they can develop internal systems of distribution. That would open the way for unprecedented prosperity, meaning rich returns for investors smart enough to have followed the transfer of purchasing power.

Desirable Industrial Sectors

Having made country selections, the next step in the top-down process would be looking at industrial sectors.

Obviously attractive would be the stocks of producers (or companies providing supporting services to producers) of the commodities or natural resources driving that country's economy.

Having made country selections, the next step in the top-down process would be looking at industrial sectors.

Stocks of electric, oil, or gas utilities companies that have predictable earnings because they can raise rates and that pay consistently high dividends would be attractive investments, as would property trusts or real estate investment trusts (REITs) invested in commercial office buildings and shopping centers (where the dividends we receive are, in practicality, rental income).

Investments in a country's infrastructure, manufacturing base, and transportation systems are additional ways to tap into the core vitality of growing economies.

A list of desirable industrial sectors would include:

Agriculture
Energy (oil and gas, coal, alternative sources)
Forestry
Infrastructure
Manufacturing

Mining (industrial raw materials, precious metals)
Property
Transportation (rail, shipping, etc.)
Utilities
Water

Some Favorite Nations

Profits on currency conversion have been the metric accounting for the largest percentage of total returns in recent years and should continue to be. Here is a breakdown of the basket of currencies I invest in for the bulk of my clients and how each fared against the U.S. dollar in the 52-week period ended April 30, 2008:

Foreign Currency Gains Vs. United States Dollar	
Australian dollar	19.41%
Norwegian krone	18.70
Euro	18.35
Swiss franc	15.07
Swedish krona	15.10
Japanese yen	12.67
Singapore dollar	12.10
Canadian dollar	11.87
Chinese yuan/renminbi	10.90
New Zealand dollar	7.80
British pound	1.48
Hong Kong dollar	0.00

Dividends from investments denominated or, in the case of China, having earnings denominated, in these currencies produced a 9.2 percent average yield.

In a larger book, I would love to give you my reasons for favoring the countries just listed. Instead, I have selected some sample countries that are representative and important and that I think you'll find interesting.

Australia

Australia is a gem. It is a large, English-speaking nation with an economy as developed as any on earth, a low unemployment rate of 4.4 percent, and a projected 2008 GDP growth rate of 3.8 percent according to International Monetary Fund (IMF) estimates, more than double the IMF projection for other developed economies like Europe and Japan. Roughly 60 percent of its exports go to Asia, making it relatively immune to the slowdown in the United States.

Australia is rich in natural resources, including raw materials like copper, lead, nickel, and zinc and agricultural commodities such as wheat. It has one of the world's largest supplies of natural gas, enough to satisfy its energy needs for the rest of this century, giving it a competitive advantage over Europe, Japan, and the United States as they and other countries struggle with skyrocketing oil prices. While other countries are creating inflation, Australia's central bank is raising interest rates to keep inflation in check.

In the 12 months ended in April 2008, the Australian dollar led the list of currencies appreciating against the U.S. dollar with a stunning gain of 19.4 percent. Add that to dividend yields that have been in a range of 10 percent to 13 percent and higher.

Australia's proximity to China positions it ideally as the major exporter of raw materials to a country where the demand will be insatiable.

Canada

In terms of area, Canada is the world's second largest country, after Russia, and is one of the world's wealthiest countries in terms of per-capita income. It is a parliamentary democracy and a constitutional monarchy, with Queen Elizabeth as its head of state, and is organized as a federation comprising 10 provinces and three territories. It is a member of the G-8, the group of eight leading industrialized countries, and one of the world's 10 leading trading nations. A party to the North American Free Trade Agreement (NAFTA), it has a substantial trade surplus with the United States, which, as its chief trading partner, absorbs 80 percent of its exports and supplies 55 percent of its imports. Canada is the largest foreign supplier of energy, including oil, gas, uranium, and electric power, to the United States.

Since World War II, rapid growth in Canada's manufacturing, mining, and service sectors has transformed it from a primarily rural economy into one that is primarily urban and industrial. Generally developing along the same lines as the United States, Canada has a similar market-oriented economic system, pattern of production, and high standard of living.

Problems with high inflation and excessive speculation in real estate during the late 1980s led to a severe recession in 1990 and 1991. After defaults, downsizings, and restructurings in the private sector and government measures aimed at reducing debt and reversing budget deficits, Canada's economic performance was markedly improved by the later 1990s, and its economy has been expanding robustly since then. It will meet the challenges posed by the economic decline of the United States from a strong position.

Canada is a resource-rich country with iron ore, nickel, zinc, copper, gold, uranium, lead, molybdenum, potash, diamonds, silver, fish, timber, coal, petroleum, natural gas, and hydropower. It is rich in agricultural products, and its chief industries include transportation equipment, chemicals, processed and unprocessed minerals, food products, wood and paper products, fish products, petroleum, and natural gas.

Singapore

Singapore is a sovereign city-state (Monaco and Vatican City are the only other remaining examples of this venerable form of government) and the smallest country in Southeast

Asia. It has been called the freest country in the world and has been rated as the world's most business-friendly economy. A CIA publication calls it a highly developed and successful free-market economy that enjoys a remarkably open and corruption-free environment, stable prices, and a per capita GDP equal to that of the four largest West European countries. Its economy depends heavily on exports, particularly in consumer electronics and information technology products. Manufacturing, however, is otherwise well diversified into petroleum refining, chemicals, mechanical engineering, and biomedical sciences.

From 2001 through 2003 Singapore's economy took a hit from the global recession, the slump in the technology sector, and an outbreak of severe acute respiratory syndrome (SARS) in 2003, which adversely affected tourism and consumer spending generally.

Thanks to fiscal stimulus, low interest rates, a surge in exports, and internal measures, 2004 through 2007 saw vigorous growth, with real GDP growth averaging 7 percent annually. The unemployment rate in 2007 was a remarkably low 1.8 percent.

Annualized growth in the first quarter of 2008 was 16.9 percent, partly reflecting major external investments in pharmaceuticals and medical technology. Efforts continue to establish Singapore as Southeast Asia's financial, high-tech, and medical tourism hub.

Singapore is the third most popular place for Chinese companies to list their stocks, after Hong Kong and the United States.

Singapore's dollar (S$) gained 12.1 percent over the U.S. dollar in the 12-month period ended April 30, 2008.

Norway

Norway is certainly one of my favorite countries, and for a lot of people it's one of the developed world's best-kept secrets. Did you know, for example, that it is one of the world's leading oil producers and that its petroleum exports are exceeded only by those of Saudi Arabia and Russia?

Norway elected to remain outside the Eurozone. Its currency, the krone, gained 18.7 percent against the U.S. dollar in the year ended April 30, 2008, second only to the Australian dollar's 19.4 percent gain. Rated the most peaceful country in the world by the *Economist* magazine, Norway also has one of the highest standards of living and an unemployment rate below 2 percent.

Here's what the CIA *World Factbook* says about Norway:

> The Norwegian economy is a prosperous bastion of welfare capitalism, featuring a combination of free market activity and government intervention. The government controls key areas, such as the vital petroleum sector, through large-scale state enterprises. The country is

richly endowed with natural resources—petroleum, hydropower, fish, forests, and minerals—with oil and gas accounting for one-third of exports.

The government has moved ahead with privatization. Although Norwegian oil production peaked in 2000, natural gas production is still rising. Norwegians realize that once their gas production peaks they will eventually face declining oil and gas revenues; accordingly Norway has been saving its oil- and gas-boosted budget surpluses in a Government Petroleum Fund, which is invested abroad and now is valued at more than $250 billion. After lackluster growth of less than 1 percent in 2002–2003, GDP growth picked up to 3–5 percent in 2004–2007, partly due to higher oil prices. Norway's economy remains buoyant. Domestic economic activity is, and will continue to be, the main driver of growth, supported by high consumer confidence and strong investment spending in the offshore oil and gas sector. Norway's record high budget surplus and upswing in the labor market in 2007 highlights the strength of its economic position going into 2008.

Norway's central bank recently raised its short-term lending rate to 5.5 percent as an anti-inflation move and indicated a further rise might be in the cards should conditions warrant it.

Hong Kong

Hong Kong was under British rule from 1842 until July 1, 1997, when it became the Hong Kong Special Administrative Region (SAR) of China. Under a 1984 Sino-British

Joint Declaration, China promised that under its "one country, two systems" policy, China's socialist economic system would not be imposed on Hong Kong, which, under a constitutional document called The Basic Law, would have a capitalist economic system, enjoy guaranteed personal rights and privileges, and have a high degree of autonomy, except in military and foreign affairs, until at least 2047, 50 years after the transfer of sovereignty.

Hong Kong is a model of laissez-faire capitalism with minimal taxation and government intervention. It is an important center for international finance and trade, and has the highest concentration of corporate headquarters in the Asia-Pacific region. The total value of its trading activity, including imports, exports, and re-exports, largely mainland products, exceeds its GDP. Its export markets are mainland China (46 percent), the United States, and Japan. During the past decade, Hong Kong's manufacturing has been moving to the mainland and its GDP is now 91 percent services. Natural resources are limited, and food and raw materials are imported.

The Hong Kong Stock Exchange is the sixth largest in the world with a market capitalization of nearly $3 trillion (U.S.), more than half of which represents mainland companies. It is the premier stock market for Chinese firms seeking to list abroad.

The Hong Kong dollar has been pegged to the U.S. dollar since 1983.

Switzerland

Switzerland voted against membership in the Eurozone in December 2002, preferring to conduct and develop its relationships with EU members and other European nations through bilateral agreements. In recent years, the Swiss have brought their economic practices largely into conformity with the EU's to enhance their international competitiveness.

The CIA *World Factbook* describes Switzerland as a peaceful, prosperous, and stable modern market economy with low unemployment (less than half the EU average), a highly skilled labor force, and a per capita GDP larger than that of the big Western European economies. It remains a safe haven for investors because of its famous secret Swiss bank accounts and because it has kept up the Swiss franc's long-term external value. Following a slow GDP growth period in the early 2000s along with the rest of Europe, Switzerland's GDP growth began picking up in 2004 and was a brisk 2.6 percent in 2007.

Switzerland's major industries are chemicals, health and pharmaceuticals, instruments, real estate, banking, and insurance. It ranks among the countries considered easiest to do business in.

New Zealand

New Zealand is a small but wealthy Pacific nation with a population of 4.2 million that in the past 20 years has been transformed from an agrarian economy dependent on concessionary British market access to a more industrialized, free-market economy that can compete globally.

The country is heavily dependent on trade, especially in agricultural products, with exports accounting for some 24 percent of its GDP, and half its exports representing agriculture, horticulture, fishing, wool, and forestry. Its major export partners are Australia (20.5 percent), the United States (13.1 percent), Japan (10.3 percent), China (5.4 percent), and the United Kingdom (4.9 percent). Its heavy dependence on agricultural exports makes New Zealand particularly sensitive to international commodity prices.

New Zealand is actively pursuing free trade agreements, and on April 7, 2008, the New Zealand China Free Trade Agreement was signed, the first such agreement China has signed with a developed country.

Economic challenges include a trade deficit of 7 to 9 percent of GDP, slow development of noncommodity exports, and lagging labor productivity growth. Brain drains have been a problem since the 1970s, but recently brain gains have added educated professionals from poorer countries and from Europe to the ranks of permanent settlers.

The New Zealand Exchange Ltd. (NZX) is a state-of-the-art stock exchange facility located in Wellington, New Zealand.

The New Zealand dollar gained 7.8 percent over the U.S. dollar in a recent 52-week period.

The Netherlands

The Netherlands has a prosperous and open market economy and is a founding member of the European Community. It depends to a large extent on foreign trade and ranks third worldwide in value of agricultural exports, behind the United States and France. It exports two-thirds of the world's total of fresh-cut plants, flowers, and bulbs; a quarter of all world tomatoes; and one-third of the world's peppers and cucumbers.

The economy is noted for stable industrial relations, moderate unemployment and inflation, a sizable current account surplus, and an important role as a European transportation hub. Its industries are mainly food processing, chemicals, petroleum refining, and electrical machinery.

One of the largest natural gas fields in the world is located in the north of the Netherlands, and with only half of its reserves used up, it is expected to benefit from the continuing rise in oil prices.

The Netherlands is a leader among European nations in attracting foreign direct investment and is one of the five largest investors in the United States.

The Amsterdam Stock Exchange, once the world's oldest, was merged on September 22, 2000, with the Brussels Stock Exchange and the Paris Stock Exchange to form Euronext and is now known as Euronext Amsterdam.

Parting Words

Country selection is the first step in my conservative strategy of buying and holding foreign securities. Putting the "where" before the "what" is known in the business as a top-down strategy, and for my money it's the only way to go in foreign investing. There, the primary objective is to get positioned in strong, growing economies whose currencies are gaining in exchange value over the U.S. dollar.

Once I decide what country I want to be in, I look for industrial sectors enjoying bull trends and then for rock-solid equity investments that will thrive as the economies thrive, enjoying earnings growth and paying high dividends that keep pace with inflation.

With the U.S. dollar expected to continue losing purchasing power, nondollar investments in earnings streams coming from nondollar sources offer the best prospect of preserving your wealth and standard of living. When the U.S. economy recovers its vibrancy, as I believe it ultimately will, you'll have the money to take advantage of promising opportunities here.

Chapter Nine

If You Want to Roll the Dice

~

The Lure of Emerging Markets

THE AMERICAN ECONOMY may be coming unglued. I'm convinced this is true, but does it make sense to invest in emerging economies, where the glue is still hardening? My answer is a complicated one, but the bottom line is yes. Investing in emerging markets is a little like riding a bucking bull, pun intended. It requires a cowboy's skill and bravery, but there's nothing quite like it, and the prize money makes it all worthwhile.

Emerging markets, which are also called developing and lesser-developed countries, are an asset class whose admission requirements include a stock market open to foreigners and providing an adequate degree of liquidity, an absence of prohibitive regulation and taxation, a unified currency, and a growing industrial base, even though the standard of living may be low. Economic potential is the defining standard. I'm not talking here about agricultural societies we know by such names as *Third World*, *underdeveloped*, or *nonindustrialized* nations.

———————————— ∾ ————————————

Because of this value as a hedge against falling stock prices and because they have been touted by mutual funds as hot investments, emerging markets have attracted growing numbers of investors seeking diversification and high returns.

As an asset class, emerging markets stocks tend to be countercyclical to both American and European stock markets and more in sync with commodity market cycles, which I suspect owes to the fact that raw materials and energy companies represent the largest single segment of the emerging markets sector. Because of this value as a hedge against falling stock prices and because they have been touted by mutual funds as hot investments, emerging markets have attracted growing numbers of investors seeking diversification and high returns.

They have also attracted a lot of hedge fund money, representing speculations and interest rate trades, and this has added greatly to their volatility.

And they have been going great guns. Since 2003, the Morgan Stanley Capital Investment (MSCI) Emerging Markets Free Index (MEF), which represents nearly 800 securities with a market value of over $1 trillion in 26 emerging economy stock markets open to foreign investors, has averaged a 25 percent annual gain, more than double the MSCI U.S. Index and substantially outperforming the MSCI Europe, Australasia, and Far East (EAFE) Index, the benchmark index of international developed markets.

That's impressive, but don't get carried away. In the 10 years leading up to 2003, the MEF had an annualized return of only 0.18 percent, according to Morningstar. By comparison, the Wilshire 5000 index of all U.S. stocks gained 9.61 percent annually, with substantially less volatility.

So the risk in emerging markets is high and takes a variety of forms, including political uncertainty, currency instability, heavy indebtedness in some cases, questionable fundamental data and research information, nonstandard or inadequate disclosure, possible enforcement difficulties, and limited remedies in the event of legal challenges.

Despite all the risks, emerging markets are indisputably the wave of the future and I'd have no hesitation in dubbing them a bull move in a bear market, provided it was clear that only professionals should play.

An Impressive Track Record

The MSCI Emerging Markets Free Index (MEF) is a proxy for emerging markets in general and includes Argentina, Brazil, Chile, China, Colombia, the Czech Republic, Greece, Hungary, India, Indonesia, Israel, Jordan, Malaysia, Mexico, Pakistan, Peru, Philippines, Poland, Russia, South Africa, South Korea, Sri Lanka, Taiwan, Thailand, Turkey, and Venezuela. The MEF's composition is a representative but not all-inclusive list of emerging markets. Other lists include African nations like Nigeria and Botswana, and six Arab states gathered as the Gulf Cooperation Council (GCC), which includes the United Arab Emirates (UAE) and its shining city-states, Abu Dhabi and Dubai. You'll see many other countries on various lists of emerging markets, and some are on the borderline of developed and developing. (I consider Thailand and the Philippines, for example, to be developed economies just a notch below the top tier, although they are in the MEF). The most inclusive classifications would probably have about 45 countries comprising something like two-thirds of the world's total population.

A quick glance at the countries making up the MEF gives you an idea of how real the currency, economic, and political risks are in this asset class. Six of the countries listed were victims of the Asian Crisis of 1997–1998. There were also Mexico's 1982 default and near default again in 1994, the collapse of Argentina's economy in 2002, Brazil's 40 percent devaluation the same year, Chile's inflationary episode in the 1970s, and Russia's default in 1998. Now we have the politicization of Venezuela's oil industry under Hugo Chavez, not to mention chronic unrest in Israel and instability in Pakistan.

Just in case you think the foregoing were isolated incidents whose effects could be eliminated through diversification, consider this: When the Mexican peso devalued in 1994, emerging markets stocks dropped 24 percent. When Thailand let its currency fall on July 2, 1997, the group fell 37 percent in six months. Russia's default in August 1998 caused a 19 percent drop in the asset class. So emerging markets are not where you'd go looking for peace of mind.

**Emerging market shares can be
bought relatively cheaply.**

However, emerging market shares can be bought relatively cheaply. On an average price-to-earnings basis, the group has been selling between 10 and 14 times earnings, while the Standard & Poor's 500 Stock Index has ranged between 18 and 21 times, and developed markets have also been significantly higher priced. Long-term returns of emerging markets stocks have averaged 1 to 2 percent above their developed counterparts.

And the gains that some of these emerging markets have registered have been phenomenal. The four largest—Brazil, Russia, India, and China—are known by the acronym BRIC. Between November 2001 and November 2007, Russia's Micex index climbed 781 percent, India's Senses soared 508 percent, and Brazil's Bovespa gained 395 percent. The MSCI China index, which includes shares subject to mainland stock ownership restrictions, rose 501 percent. Compare those figures with those of non–United States developed markets, which merely doubled during the period, and with the Standard & Poor's 500 Stock Index, which gained a paltry 32 percent.

If the emerging markets have been more sensitive to the problems of neighboring emerging markets, they have been less affected by problems in developed economies. In the week following the first reports of bank writedowns on credit losses in late 2007, the S&P 500 Stock Index in the United States stocks dropped 1.7 percent, but three of the four BRIC markets showed gains ranging from 0.3 percent to 3.8 percent. Only the Bovespa had a 0.4 percent loss.

I recently read a reprint of an article that appeared in *U.S. News & World Report*, dated October 11, 2007, by Emily Brandon, that posed and answered the question, "Is the world's economy tipping in favor of emerging markets?"

> No question about it. Ten years ago, we had the Asia Financial Crisis. Today we have the American financial crisis. Then, those countries had to be bailed out. Today, emerging markets sit on 75 percent of the world's foreign exchange reserves. They were dependent on the West for money, for management, for everything. Today, we would not be able to function without oil from the Middle East. Our interest rates would be higher without the Chinese to buy our Treasury bills. Yes, the world has really changed and is tipping in favor of emerging markets in the sense that you have a group of what used to be very poor countries slowly becoming middle class. We overconsume, and we underinvest. They underconsume and overinvest. They help us make up the difference between what we save, which is not enough, and what we invest, which is also not enough. They help us keep our standard of living.

I couldn't have put it better myself, and would only observe that since that article was written, our standard of living has already begun to transfer from us to them. This is a process that I am convinced will continue.

How Do I Ride This Emerging Bull?

If you are a conservative, risk-averse investor not so keen on riding bucking bulls, be assured that the trends that make the emerging markets dynamic—the realignment of purchasing power, the industrialization of India and China, and the consequent demand for natural resources, raw materials, and commodities—can be played safely and profitably using a buy-and-hold strategy with high-yielding stocks in developed countries, as prescribed in Chapter 7. You don't have to invest directly in mainland China to profit from its projected growth when more established companies in Hong Kong and Singapore do so much business there. Also, countries like Australia, a stable, developed country in close proximity, is a major exporter satisfying China's ravenous appetite for raw materials.

The greatest returns reward the greatest risk, and the most money will be made by people who invest in emerging markets directly.

But the greatest returns reward the greatest risk, and the most money will be made by people who invest in emerging markets directly.

One way to do that is through ADRs sponsored by companies in emerging markets, such as Samsung, a household name and the largest conglomerate in South Korea. There are others, but the same objections I voiced in Chapter 7 to ADRs apply here.

A better choice would be exchange-traded funds (ETFs) that represent emerging markets indexes. I discussed ETFs and their pros and cons in Chapters 5 though 7, and you might want to review those sections.

The most conservative emerging markets ETFs are those that replicate total market indexes, such as iShares MSCI Emerging Markets Index Fund (EEM), Power-Shares FTSE RAFI Emerging Markets Portfolio (PXH), SPDR S&P Emerging Markets ETF (GMM), and Vanguard Emerging Markets ETF (VWO).

Somewhat less conservative are multiregion emerging markets ETFs, such as iShares MSCI BRIC Index Fund (BKF) and SPDR S&P BRIC 40 ETF (BIK) (formerly streetTRACKS Index Shares).

After that are ETFs specializing in regions, such as Latin America, Europe, and Middle East/Africa. Such narrow exposure would obviously mean unacceptable risk to an individual planning to buy and hold. But for an investor with expertise in emerging markets, buying separate ETFs representing different regions or markets

would permit selective trading with the added profit
potential that that might provide.

～

**Anyone with expertise in emerging markets, or
with access to an adviser having such specialized
expertise, will do best with a selected portfolio of
individual stocks bought directly on the
exchanges in the emerging economies.**

Of course, anyone with expertise in emerging markets, or with access to an adviser having such specialized
expertise, will do best with a selected portfolio of individual stocks bought directly on the exchanges in the emerging economies. As with developed markets, you would
need a specialized broker and should follow the guidelines
set forth in Chapter 5.

Probably the most sensible alternative for serious
nonprofessional investors would be a managed account
with a broker-adviser. A managed account is an arrangement whereby one or more investors entrust a professional, such as Euro Pacific Capital or a similarly
specialized firm, to make investment decisions on a discretionary basis for a management fee. In the hands of a

skilled professional, a managed account should be able to play this dramatic upward trend with maximum profitability while minimizing volatility.

Parting Words

The asset class known as *emerging markets* comprises the 25 to 50 countries in Eastern Europe, Asia, Africa, and South America that are on the cusp of industrial revolution and represent the vanguard of global economic growth in the future. It is a group that represents the most exciting prospects for wealth accumulation but also has the greatest amount of currency, economic, and political risk.

I think every nondollar portfolio should have a prudent degree of exposure to this highly dynamic asset class, but I believe it is an area where expertise is absolutely vital. Participation through exchange-traded equity index funds having broad geographical representation is a convenient, relatively low-cost alternative for investors of modest means, provided they are prepared for a high degree of volatility. The best solution, I believe, is a managed fund with a financial adviser specializing in foreign markets.

Chapter Ten

To Infinity and Beyond

~

Secure Employment for the Future

BAD TIMES ARE COMING for working Americans. In the next few years, millions of people who believe that they are secure in their jobs will be shocked to discover they're not.

When I wrote this chapter in the summer of 2008, the U.S. job outlook was increasingly grim. Official U.S. unemployment had recently jumped from 5 percent to 5.5 percent in one month—the biggest such increase in more than 20 years.

That sounds bad, but reality is even worse. As I explained in Chapters 2 and 3, the government uses incomplete statistics to mislead the public about inflation, measuring it with a carefully selected basket of items that it subjectively alters to minimize any increases. It excludes from that basket food and energy, two items that everyone needs but that might annoy the government by increasing in price quickly, dispelling the low-inflation myth.

The government uses similar subterfuge when it measures unemployment, counting only those people who have actively applied for jobs within the previous four weeks. That leaves out millions who have (1) become discouraged and given up their job hunt; (2) despaired of finding a job and are trying to start a business instead; (3) gone into early retirement because of the dismal job prospects for anyone over 50; or (4) are underemployed, working part-time or temporary jobs because they can't find full-time, permanent employment. If you include those who've given up looking for work—as the government should—I estimate the real unemployment rate to be closer to 10 percent.

I've predicted for years that the coming collapse of the U.S. economy would bring down some of its seemingly strongest industries. Today, that prediction is starting to come true, and every week brings new announcements of massive layoffs at previously solid companies. United

Airlines, the nation's second-largest carrier, is laying off 1,600 employees, and Continental, its fourth-largest, is laying off 3,000. Both Ford and General Motors are also planning massive layoffs, and even mainstream analysts are now talking of bankruptcy. (Of course, when I pointed this out a few years ago, my warnings were readily dismissed as too farfetched to be taken seriously.)

The pain isn't limited to airlines and automakers. Some of the most venerable names in the financial industry are feeling the effect of hard times—or, more accurately, suffering the consequences of their own greed. That's what happened to Bear Stearns, the investment bank and brokerage house that was founded in 1923 and survived the stock market crash of 1929 without laying off a single employee. In 2008, its 85-year history came to a close with an ignominious bailout, followed by a forced sale to JPMorgan Chase.

Lehman Brothers, founded in 1850, posted its first quarterly loss in 2008 since going public in 1994—and it was a *big* loss: $2.8 billion. To try to dispel rumors that it will soon go the way of Bear Stearns, Lehman is rapidly raising money and laying off employees, more than 5,000 of them in the past year.

Things are going to get worse—much, much worse—before they get better. Within the next few years, Americans will face a job market they no longer recognize. Much of today's workforce is too young to remember the days when the economy rose and fell on its own, without the federal government borrowing foreign funds to create so-called stimulus measures, thus avoiding normal market corrections. As foreign sources of credit dry up, the government will be powerless to stop the coming economic collapse. I foresee many industries severely contracting or dying altogether, taking millions of jobs with them. It will be a very bad time to find yourself out of work.

If you start following my advice right now, however, you can protect yourself from the worst of the downturn. You can even take advantage of unique opportunities that the coming decade will offer—to those few who have the smarts to be ready for them. Read on to find out which industries and professions will suffer the most, and which hold out promising hopes for growth and advancement.

Service without a Smile

In the past 30 years or so, our government and business leaders collectively shot the U.S. economy in the foot by encouraging a major transition from a manufacturing-based economy to a service-based one. Today, more than two-thirds of the U.S. gross domestic product (GDP) is produced in the service sector.

Many U.S. residents see this as a good thing, and no wonder. A service economy has many lifestyle advantages for the people living in it. There are no smokestacks to interfere with the view from million-dollar-mortgaged homes, and no need to follow a demanding factory schedule. College graduates with useless humanities degrees can always find work pushing pencils in an accounting, legal, or financial firm. Best of all, no more calluses on hands or aching muscles from the physical labor many factory and agricultural jobs require. Plus production jobs are capital intensive, requiring major investments in plant and equipment; service sector jobs, by contrast, require relatively little in the way of capital—perfect for a nation devoid of savings. It sounds like a good deal, but there's a basic problem. Just as an individual can't survive by only consuming and never producing anything, so the United States in the global economy must produce as well as consume. The only way to do this is to export, and services, for the most part, can't be exported. This is why, along with our two-thirds service economy, the United States has a trade deficit of approximately $60 billion *per month*.

—————— ❧ ——————

As that easy credit dries up, there won't be any way to continue funding the purchase of these services.

We have no one but ourselves to be customers for our services. That was no problem as long as easy credit from abroad translated into unbridled consumer spending here at home. But as that easy credit dries up, there won't be any way to continue funding the purchase of these services.

As Americans are forced to curtail their spending, demand will fall sharply for services like manicures, therapy sessions, and legal advice. That means U.S. citizens who work in the service sector—which is to say, most of us—will be the first to feel the effect of the coming collapse, and will also be the hardest hit.

Let's take a closer look at how the coming collapse will affect some once-mighty industries.

Real Estate

As I predicted, the real estate market is currently in free fall. Subprime borrowers with adjustable-rate mortgages are finding they can no longer stay in the homes they shouldn't have been allowed to buy in the first place.

Home prices have declined 35 percent or more in some overbuilt urban markets. Real estate experts, who once assured willing buyers that they would never lose money by investing in property, now say that homes in some areas will see their prices go down by 50 percent or more.

This is frightening not only because millions of Americans have been counting on the equity in their homes to see them through their retirement years, but also because in the boom years, real estate, along with related industries such as construction, pumped new jobs into an economy that was losing jobs elsewhere. The continuing real estate collapse will mean fewer jobs for all these sectors: real estate brokers, architects, mortgage bankers, appraisers, and architects. It also means fewer home-building jobs—but those in the construction industry may have new opportunities and options elsewhere. (For more about this, read on.)

Finance and Banking

These industries have long been the nation's most lucrative, accounting for just over 6 percent of employment, but more than 20 percent of corporate profits, according to figures from the Bureau of Labor Statistics and the Bureau of Economic Analysis. Many people believed a job in a financial firm would guarantee solid earnings for life, but thousands of former Bear Stearns and Lehman Brothers employees now know better.

These firms and many others have fallen victim to their managers' greed in financing the subprime mortgage market. But what about the rest of the industry? Although I foresee ongoing opportunities in financial services (which is my own area of endeavor), U.S. citizens will have less money to invest and will be more inclined to put what money they do have into savings accounts, certificates of deposit, and other boring but safe instruments. Also, as credit becomes increasingly scarce, more transactions will be effected in cash or simply not done at all, meaning fewer jobs in all aspects of consumer lending. So, this once unassailable industry will continue to lose jobs.

In addition, after wiping out shareholder equity and dispensing lousy investment advice to its clients, Wall Street's reputation is now in shambles. A string of record bonuses, on activities that ultimately produced horrific losses for shareholders, has exposed Wall Street as placing its own personal interests above those of shareholders. Further, the bad investment advice routinely dispensed has left its clients faring not much better. My guess is this industry, like others we once dominated, will head east. After all, since that is where most of the capital is being formed and invested, and given our tarnished reputation, it really makes little sense for the world to outsource the allocation process to New York.

Retail

The retail industry is a particularly vulnerable part of the service economy. Over the past 20 years, the greatest growth in this sector has been in national chains of big-box retail stores, which usually operate with thin profit margins. This business model is built on cheap imports from other countries, most notably China, whose careful control of the yuan-dollar exchange rate has kept prices artificially low. But imported goods will become scarcer and more expensive just when Americans have less disposable income to shop with and little, if any, access to credit to make up the difference. When that happens, many big boxes will find themselves empty of customers. This could be particularly bad news if you happen to work for Wal-Mart, the largest private employer in the world.

Health Care

This is one segment of the service economy where most prognosticators consistently predict endless growth. Their logic goes like this: Baby Boomers are aging; people are living longer. This adds up to a rapidly expanding population of elderly citizens who will need more and more care as they age. Meanwhile, constant medical advances mean there are more treatments than ever before, more ways to manage serious illnesses, and more people living longer with diseases, which once again will lead to more elderly people needing yet more care.

There's only one problem with this forecast: We can't afford it. Neither the United States as a nation nor our citizens as individuals will be able to pay for ever more complex, expensive, and protracted health care treatments. Today, more and more working Americans are paying for their own health insurance and medical treatment because employers can no longer afford to do so.

One result has been high-deductible health plans that require patients to pay the first $1,000 or more of their health care expenses out of pocket. These plans come with an option for a health savings account in which the insured will supposedly set aside money for medical expenses—but we've all seen how good we are at saving. Instead, the likely result will be more people buying high-deductible plans (because that's all they can afford) and then forgoing medical care altogether because they can't come up with the deductible.

In the face of these harsh realities, legislators on both sides of the aisle have begun calling for universal health coverage, but that won't solve the problem either. The government doesn't have enough money to provide health care for all Americans, and it won't be able to keep borrowing. The only way to pay for universal health coverage would be to heavily tax a populace that is already reeling from economic setbacks, an idea that's sure to be deeply unpopular. Indeed, in the coming years, the government will have a hard time funding Medicare and Medicaid, the two national health plans already in place.

With dwindling government funding and U.S. residents financially squeezed, the industry will inevitably contract. I predict there will be fewer health care jobs, not more, over the coming decade. There will likely be growth in patients from foreign countries traveling to the United States for medical procedures that will become more affordable in their own currencies as the dollar continues to decline. But it won't be enough to make up the shortfall left by Americans who can no longer pay their medical bills.

In the end, it may not be the quality of health care that contracts, but the quantity, as a poorer United States seeks to economize and some of the excesses get wrung out of this bloated system. For that to happen, however, the government will have to get out of the health care business and return this important segment of our economy to the private sector, subject to free-market forces— where it should have been all along.

Travel and Tourism

As layoffs in the airline industry demonstrate, travel and tourism are already being affected by the unfolding economic collapse. This sector is squeezed between falling demand, due to U.S. residents' reduced discretionary income, and rising oil prices due to the falling dollar. (*Staycation* is the new catchphrase for staying home during time off from work because one can no longer afford to travel.)

The bright spot for the travel and tourism industry is in destination cities and attractions that draw foreign visitors. As the dollar continues to drop and standards of living in countries like China, Russia, and India improve, more foreigners will spend their vacations in the United States. They may fill some of the airline seats and hotel rooms left vacant by staycationing locals. In addition, as U.S. residents curtail their foreign travel, citizens of emerging markets, previously too poor to travel, will quickly fill the void. So while fewer U.S. residents will be spending their summers in Europe, there will be plenty of Chinese, Indians, Russians, and others strolling the Champs-Élysées in their place.

Rebuilding the United States

The coming changes will be terribly painful, but not for everyone. As the service economy recedes, the United States will have no choice but to rebuild its manufacturing base, shore up its crumbling infrastructure, and support those few industries where it remains a world leader. That should mean both opportunities and job security for those astute enough to get into those industries now, while they still have a choice. I foresee the following as the 10 strongest professions and industries over the coming decade and beyond:

1. *Engineering*. It will take many years and a lot of effort to retool the United States's abandoned industrial base for twenty-first-century manufacturing. Engineers of all sorts—mechanical, electrical, computer science—will be needed to get the job done.

2. *Construction*. As I mentioned earlier, the collapsing real estate economy has knocked the legs out from under new home and office construction. But for those individuals and firms that can make the transition to building or rebuilding America's roads, bridges, tunnels, public transportation systems, communication lines, and the rest of our infrastructure, there should be plenty of opportunity for the foreseeable future.

The United States will have no choice but to rebuild its manufacturing base, shore up its crumbling infrastructure, and support those few industries where it remains a world leader.

---

3. *Agriculture*. Right now we import a surprising amount of the food we eat from other countries, and also export soybeans, wheat, and other foodstuffs. As imports become prohibitively expensive, the United States will have no choice but to grow

and raise more of its own food. At the same time, as the dollar falls and we struggle to redress the trade imbalance, exports of all descriptions will become vitally important. This should spell opportunity in the agricultural arena for years to come.

4. *Merchant marine.* If you like the idea of an adventurous life on the high seas, consider a career in the merchant marine or commercial fishing. The United States has allowed its merchant marine to dwindle to next to nothing in regard to both its personnel and its fleet, with many former U.S. ships reflagged under other nationalities to avoid dealing with U.S. regulations and to take advantage of lower labor costs overseas. But U.S. labor costs will decline over the coming decade, while hiring foreign workers becomes ever more expensive in dollar terms as the dollar declines. Meanwhile, an increase in the export of U.S. goods should create more demand for shipping.

The combination should lead to a growing need for mariners, and the profession has several advantages. First, you get to see the world, which may be helpful if you decide at some point to relocate to another country as the U.S. economy collapses. (For more on this, see Chapter 12.) Second, you'll have easier access to what will soon be unaffordable imported goods. And you will have an international occupation that can be practiced nearly anywhere in the world.

5. *Commercial fishing*. Commercial fishing and fish farming should be another growth industry that allows for a secure future, although not as much as international travel. Currently, the United States imports about 90 percent of the fish it consumes. This can't continue, because as the dollar drops, foreign labor costs rise, and the oceans continue to be denuded of fish, prices for imported seafood will become prohibitive for most American consumers.

Meanwhile, demand for fish is growing as the United States ages and becomes both more health-conscious and more sophisticated in its tastes. Unless U.S. residents give up eating fish, more of it will need to be caught and farmed in our home waters, so I predict growth in commercial fishing and fish farming over the years to come.

6. *Energy*. As I've stated elsewhere, the rising price of oil is really an effect of the dollar's decline—as each dollar loses value, it takes more of them to purchase a barrel of oil. But whatever the cause, price increases for all forms of energy are creating opportunities that will get only better as oil, gas, and coal prices continue to escalate. Consider any career related to wind generation, solar energy, and nuclear energy, and also rebuilding our oil refineries.

7. *Computers and high technology*. This U.S. industry has remained solid despite the collapse of other manufacturing sectors. The United States continues to be a world leader in computer manufacture, and this field should continue to provide opportunities for years to come.

8. *Entertainment*. If there's one thing every nation on earth makes sure to import from the United States, it's our Hollywood productions, both movies and television programming. As the dollar continues its decline, it will be ever more affordable for overseas customers to purchase our entertainment products, or even use U.S. production facilities and talent to create entertainment products of their own.

   I'm obviously not suggesting you pursue a career as a Hollywood star, but there are any number of behind-the-scenes jobs, such as video editing, lighting, cinematography, production management, and so on, that can provide solid careers for many years to come. My one caveat is that foreign tastes for U.S. pop culture could diminish as the United States loses its status as an economic world leader. So make sure to keep an eye on foreign audiences and responses if you go into this field.

9. *Automotive repair, small appliance repair, and the like*. The U.S. habit of buying or leasing a new car

every few years will go by the wayside as incomes shrink and prices increase. U.S. residents will be keeping their cars on the road for many years longer, and the same principle will apply to other expensive items as well. So anyone who knows how to fix things, from carburetors to toaster ovens to torn leather upholstery, should see demand for these skills grow over the coming years.

10. *Tailoring and textiles.* If you looked in the closets and drawers of most U.S. residents today, it would be a challenge to find even one article of clothing made in the United States. But rising prices will soon cut off the flow of inexpensive clothing items from overseas, and U.S. residents will have to get out of the habit of simply throwing away an item of clothing because it's torn, worn, or out of fashion. This will mean a growing need for tailoring and clothing repair, as well as shoe and leather goods repair.

Imported clothes will be both scarcer and more expensive, but U.S. residents will, of course, still need to clothe themselves. This will necessarily lead to a revival of the United States's abandoned clothing manufacturing industry, which should provide secure employment for years to come.

Major Decisions

If you or your children are heading to college (or returning to college), consider the preceding information carefully when choosing an academic major. During the years that the United States was dominated by a service economy, it didn't really matter if students graduated with degrees in political science, communications, or other liberal arts. There was always some sort of clerical or administrative work to be found.

With the service economy withering and the U.S. job market shrunken, those options will no longer exist by the time today's students become graduates. For some, trade school might offer a more useful—and much less expensive—alternative. For others, a degree in a practical field such as engineering, geology, animal husbandry, or computer science will provide a fighting chance at a good job in the tough years to come. In addition, don't neglect the foreign languages portion of your education. Becoming fluent in Mandarin Chinese, Japanese, Arabic, Hindi, or Russian will be quite helpful to your future job prospects.

Parting Words

Has this chapter frightened you? I hope the answer is yes, especially if you work in the service economy. The employment landscape a few years from now will bear no resemblance to what most Americans have grown accustomed to. Jobs are disappearing fast, and now may be your last chance to make the changes that will prepare you for dependable employment in the future.

Today, the service sector makes up more than two-thirds of the gross domestic product, but that situation can't last because for the most part the only customers for the services U.S. citizens provide are other U.S. residents. As the economy contracts and most people find themselves with less disposable income, demand for many of those services will evaporate.

With thousands of layoffs announced as this book was going to press, the airline, financial, and real estate industries are already struggling to adapt to the new economic order. Retail will soon follow suit, and its downfall will be worsened as today's inexpensive Chinese goods become pricier and scarcer in the future.

But some U.S. industries, including high tech and entertainment, have remained strong, despite the overall switch to service. And other professions and industries are destined to grow as the United States rebuilds its abandoned manufacturing base and sagging infrastructure. Engineering, geology, architecture, agriculture, construction, repair, and energy (both traditional and alternative) should offer job security and solid opportunities for the future. Make the transition to these areas now, while you still have a choice, and you will reap the benefits for many years to come.

Chapter Eleven

A Decade of Frugality

~

Making It with Less Money

AMERICANS ARE IN for some surprises—and not pleasant ones—in the next few years. The decade from 2010 to 2020 will be a period of severe adjustment for the U.S. economy, and even more so for U.S. citizens themselves. U.S. residents are accustomed to the perks of living in the world's wealthiest nation, but as I have shown throughout this book, this is no longer the case, not by a long shot. We are now living in the world's biggest debtor nation. Sooner or later, U.S. lifestyles will have to adjust to this new reality.

The Cause . . .

I've been sounding a warning for years about the huge adjustment both U.S. residents as individuals and the United States as a nation will have to make when the seemingly endless supply of foreign credit dries up. This has in fact already begun and continued to gather further momentum after this book came out. As I explained previously, the dollar is losing value against other world currencies, a trend that will continue as a result of the loss of our industrial base, the decay of our infrastructure, ongoing levels of consumer debt, and huge trade and current account imbalances.

The dollar's downward slide is painful not only for U.S. residents as their purchasing power erodes both at home and abroad, but also for our foreign creditors, who have watched their investments in the United States lose value when measured in their own currencies. Those losses are starkly worse if they invested in mortgage-backed securities, or other structured products where outright default or loss of dollar principal only compounds their foreign exchange losses. Foreign investors are feeling the pain of having bet on the dollar and the U.S. market. Sooner or later, they're going to pull the plug, and when they do its our economy that will go down the drain.

That will bring some big changes for average Americans. Depending on whose statistics you believe, U.S. households currently owe an average of $2,000 to $9,000 or more in credit card debt. Most carry that debt indefinitely by only making minimum monthly payments. In fact, when we need more cash, it's become common practice to apply for new credit cards, roll over balances, or borrow against the house (if equity still exists or the home hasn't been lost to foreclosure).

Most of this easy borrowing is ultimately backed by foreign investors, who buy the paper from U.S. financial institutions. So when foreign investors start taking their money elsewhere, the supply of easy credit will abruptly dry up, not only for the federal government, but for U.S. consumers as well.

I've been saying for years that the U.S. real estate market was a bubble looking for a pin, and that prices would collapse when easy credit disappeared. We could already see this prediction coming true when I wrote this chapter. It is much more difficult to obtain a home equity loan or mortgage today than it was even a few months ago, and no-income-verification loans are rightly becoming a thing of the past.

———————— ∾ ————————

**As credit is drying up, U.S. residents will
discover that whatever cash they *can* lay their
hands on buys much less than it once did.**

———————————————————————

Credit card companies will soon follow suit, with higher
interest rates, lower spending limits, and much more strin-
gent requirements before customers can qualify for a card
at all. Retailers who now routinely provide large amounts of
credit will curtail their offerings as well. "Pay nothing for
the first 12 months!" and other common no-money-down
deals of today will soon be quaint relics of the past.

Just as credit is drying up, U.S. residents will discover
that whatever cash they *can* lay their hands on buys much
less than it once did. This will happen for two reasons.
First, as I explained in Chapters 2 and 3, despite appear-
ances to the contrary, inflation is a real problem in the
United States. The consumer price index and producer
price index that the media and government use to measure inflation do not reflect the real changes in costs most
U.S. residents are already experiencing. As I finished
this chapter, the federal government's way of measuring
inflation, as measured by the consumer price index, was 5
percent annually. But anyone who's bought anything
lately knows prices are going up faster than they were a

few years ago. My estimate is that actual inflation is somewhere between 7 and 10 percent.

Even beyond the effects of inflation, U.S. residents will find themselves paying much higher prices for items imported from abroad—everything from a bunch of grapes to a sweater to a big-screen television. As the dollar continues to lose value against foreign currency, prices will naturally rise, and the rise will accelerate as traditionally deprived consumers in nations like China and India begin raising their own living standards. (Growing consumption in China and India, fueled by excess money creation, helped push the price of oil near a record $140 a barrel as this book was being written, though it may be higher by the time you are reading it.) There will be more dollars chasing a limited supply of goods.

Rising prices will not just be limited to imports. Prices for all goods still produced in the United States but that are capable of being exported will also rise in price.

Rising prices will not just be limited to imports. Prices for all goods still produced in the United States but that are capable of being exported will also rise in price. That is because strengthening foreign currencies will give foreign consumers an edge, enabling them to outbid U.S. residents for their own production. Domestic producers, seeking to maximize profits, will sell more of their goods abroad. If U.S. residents still want to partake, they will have to pay up to compete.

In fact, it's not just the stuff we produce that will rise in price, but the prices of many used consumer goods that we previously imported will also rise. For example, U.S. residents have a lot of cars, while the Chinese have relatively few. As the dollar plunges and the yuan soars, demand for cars will rise in China as it falls in the United States. With U.S. residents struggling to make ends meet, they will find a vibrant market in China for the cars they can no longer afford to drive. This foreign demand will drive up the prices of used goods and reverse a dynamic that has been in effect for years. Vast quantities of consumer goods will flow abroad, while a flood of dollars washes back up on our shores. In effect, our foreign suppliers will be repossessing the goods that they sold us on credit.

. . . And the Effect

For most Americans, these changes will add up to one thing: a big adjustment in the standard of living most have grown accustomed to. With the supply of easy credit drying up and prices rising ever more swiftly, most will simply have to make do with less of everything. This will mean putting off vacations or camping in the back yard, taking public transportation to work instead of driving, and putting off discretionary purchases in general.

Nowhere will this newly changed lifestyle be more evident than in average Americans' travel habits. When I wrote this chapter, the U.S. airline industry was undergoing unprecedented consolidation and posting record losses. Unfortunately, with the cost of building, servicing, and especially fueling aircraft on the rise, airlines in the United States currently supply more flights and passenger miles than U.S. consumers can afford to buy. Today, most flights are close to fully booked, and that might look like good news for the airline industry. But the fact is, even these full flights are not profitable, given today's low airfares. The only option the industry has is to substantially raise the cost of their fares and other services and cut down the number of flights in the face of falling demand.

As U.S. residents struggle to pay for the basics they could once easily afford, they'll be forced to cut out most or all discretionary spending. The unfortunate effect will be to slow demand, especially for services, which are difficult or impossible to sell abroad and now make up all but a third of the U.S. gross domestic product (GDP). I foresee that a reduced market for services means that many Americans in service professions will find themselves out of work, making our economic problems even worse.

No longer citizens of the world's wealthiest creditor nation, they are now citizens of its biggest debtor, though most continue to act as if the rest of the world bows to the United States' economic might.

In the next few years, I believe U.S. citizens will undergo a profound identity crisis. No longer citizens of the world's wealthiest creditor nation, they are now citizens of its biggest debtor, though most continue to act as if the rest of the world bows to the United States' economic might. In the 1930s, the Great Depression affected not only the United States but nearly every nation on earth, so hard times here were matched by hard times elsewhere. This time it will be different. Even the most uninformed U.S. citizens will be forced to notice that other nations' living standards are on the rise, just as ours is on the decline. This may finally force them to realize just how badly the United States has lost ground as an economic power—and how much work it will take to dig ourselves out of this gigantic economic hole.

I fervently hope that this economic crisis will be the dose of shock therapy needed to transform the United States from a nation of borrowers back to the nation of savers it once was, and that by the time the 2020s roll around, the United States will once again be an economic world leader of which its citizens can be justly proud.

In the meantime, there's a decade of frugality ahead of us. With advance planning, and some financial discipline, you can weather the downturn much better than most of your neighbors. Here's how to get ready.

Start Saving Now—But Not in Dollars

In the past few years, the United States has crossed over from a positive to a negative savings rate. That is, U.S. residents on average have begun spending more money than they earn, eating away the savings they once had or, worse, building up more and more debt, rather than setting money aside for the future. The last time this happened was during the Great Depression, when people had to tap into their savings or go into debt merely to survive.

For most U.S. residents today, spending more than they earn is not a matter of survival but a matter of lifestyle and bad habits, brought about by decades of artificially propped-up markets—first the stock market and then the real estate market. Runaway gains in stock and real estate prices made setting money aside seem like a waste of time and effort since appreciating values of investment and ever-rising home equity could be counted on to provide future wealth. Why put $20 a week into a savings or investment account and wind up with just over $1,000 a year later if, during that same year, you expect your house to gain $100,000 or more in value?

That kind of thinking has gotten millions of U.S. residents into what will be deep trouble when they discover that neither their homes nor their stock market portfolios have gained as much real value as they expected, as costs for daily necessities have risen much faster than they thought possible. One of my most disheartening predictions is that a substantial number of U.S. citizens who are currently retired will find themselves forced to return to the work force, as their pensions, Social Security, and savings prove inadequate to live on.

Don't let this happen to you. Instead, try some of these savings tactics:

- *Take advantage of automatic deductions.* Most banks now offer some form of automatic deduction plan that allows you to transfer a small sum of money to a savings account on a weekly or monthly basis. Use plans like these to painlessly set aside money that will be there later on when you need it. But once it's in your savings account, do not leave it there!

Your hard-earned savings will lose value as inflation rises and the dollar declines. Instead, use the
advice in this *Little Book* and invest that money in
foreign countries, in silver or gold, or in commodities, all of which are likely to appreciate, even as
the U.S. economy takes a beating.

- *Look for small ways to build savings.* Look around your
home. If you're like most U.S. residents, it's full of
items that you bought but don't use. Today's world
offers more opportunities to turn unused items into
cash than ever before. Clothing can be gathered up
and brought to a consignment shop (have things
clean and pressed, and on hangers, to get the best
prices). Other unused goods can be sold at a garage
sale or at an online marketplace such as eBay. Books
you no longer need can go to used book stores, or
you can sell them directly to other readers through
craigslist and other web sites.

  And don't forget to empty your pocket change
daily into a jar, bowl, or piggy bank. You'll be
surprised how quickly that can add up to big
money.

- *Don't spend that raise or bonus!* Next time you get a
compensation increase, don't spend it, or at least
not all of it. If you were able to meet your expenses
at your previous salary, you should be able to set

aside at least some portion of the increase and add it to your savings. Use automatic deductions to move some of your new paycheck into your savings account—but again, don't leave it there!

- *Look for simple ways to cut costs.* There's been a lot of discussion in the press and in personal finance books as to how buying a simple cup of coffee rather than a fancy Italian concoction—or better yet, making your own coffee—can add up to big savings over time. But coffee isn't the only case where small adjustments can snowball into real savings. Reexamine your long-distance charges, your cell phone plan, your cable or satellite TV plans. (Internet video services may offer a wider range of choices at a much lower cost.) Find out if bundling video, phone, and Internet service could reduce your monthly bills.

Keep savings in mind when you shop for large items like televisions or computers—and consider buying these and other items secondhand instead of brand-new. As the economy worsens, I predict more people will be forced to sell their valuable purchases just to stay afloat, which should create some opportunities to get real bargains. Put the money you save over buying the item new into a dollar-proof investment, and watch it grow.

Get Rid of Debt—Especially Variable-Rate Debt

Imagine you are standing in an appliance store, trying to decide whether to buy a new stereo system. The clerk explains: "I can't tell you exactly how much you will wind up paying for this system, but I know it will definitely be more than the price on the price tag."

~

Reducing or eliminating credit card debt should be one of your top priorities as you prepare for the coming economic downturn.

Would you go ahead and buy it? You may not think so. But that's exactly what you are doing every time you charge a purchase to a credit card, unless you're among the minority of U.S. citizens who pay their balances in full every month. Reducing or eliminating credit card debt should be one of your top priorities as you prepare for the coming economic downturn. This means working to aggressively pay down balances, and resisting the temptation to open new credit card (or retail store) accounts that will soon build new balances of their own. Don't roll debt over from one credit card to another to capture a low introductory rate. And don't get sucked into the common trap of using a home equity loan or line of credit to pay off credit cards. The lower interest rate may make this seem like a good idea, but unless you destroy your credit cards at the same time, the end result will likely be even more debt than you had before.

Truly taming credit card debt requires a mental adjustment similar to the one I've prescribed for the United States as a whole. We need to return to a mind-set of saving up to buy the things we want, rather than charging them now and figuring out how to pay for them later. Adopting that new mind-set will carry real economic benefits. Let's say you save up to buy a new $500 sofa. Because your money will earn interest while you're saving it, and that interest will compound over time, you may wind up actually spending only $450 by the time the sofa arrives in your home. If you charge it to a credit card, you'll have the sofa sooner, but at a much higher cost, perhaps as high as $800 once interest (and late charges, if you ever miss a payment) is taken into account. The time to make that adjustment is now. I predict, as the economy worsens, credit card companies will start charging interest rates that make today's 25 percent seem cheap, or more likely just refuse to lend altogether.

———————— ∾ ————————

We need to return to a mind-set of saving up to buy the things we want, rather than charging them now and figuring out how to pay for them later.

Credit cards may not be the only variable-rate loans in your life. If you have an adjustable rate mortgage, home equity loan, student loan, or any other variable-rate debt, the time to do something about it is now, while you still can. In the next few months or year, the weakening dollar, combined with growing foreign purchasing power, will force inflation up, and interest rates up with it. I recommend refinancing mortgages and home equity loans at a fixed rate as soon as you can. Student loans are more difficult, but there are companies whose business is built on consolidating student loans and providing a nonadjustable rate.

As a general rule, it's a bad idea to borrow for daily necessities such as clothing or food, or for luxuries such as a vacation. But it may be a good idea to borrow for something that will allow you to increase your income, such as a professional course or conference, or a car (but not a luxury car) that will allow you to get back and forth to your workplace.

By this same logic, I do recommend borrowing against the equity in your home *if* you can meet the following two conditions:

1. The rate of interest is low enough so that you can invest the money and get a higher rate of return.
2. That return is paid on a regular basis, so that you can use those dividends or other funds to make the

payments on the loan. Since you're paying your loan in dollars, if you invest abroad and the dollar continues to fall, that difference will grow into quite a tidy sum that you collect on a monthly or quarterly basis. You can pocket that difference—or better yet, add it to your savings. If, as I predict, the real estate market continues its decline, you might not be able to find a buyer for your home—so borrowing may be the only way to get any value out of it.

Stockpile Goods

If a box of corn flakes costs $3 today and $4 a year from now, then buying those corn flakes a year early provides a 33.3 percent return on investment. That compares favorably to even the most aggressive stock portfolio. So, storage space permitting, it makes sense to buy ahead and in bulk quantities anything from canned soup to laundry detergent to motor oil that you know you will need in future years, when prices are almost certain to be much higher. (Please always check expiration dates and storage recommendations for temperature and so forth, of any item you plan to stockpile.)

It might even make sense to stockpile some items you yourself don't use. For instance, wine, liquor, cigarettes, and cigars don't lose quality over time, if you can provide them with an appropriate environment, and might even improve as they mature. As prices skyrocket and Asian consumers begin buying more luxury goods, products such as these can become very valuable barter items— worth much, much more than the price you pay for them today. A carton of cigarettes that costs $15 in today's market might be worth $30 a couple of years from now. Now that's a return on investment!

It might also be a good idea to buy a handgun and lots of extra ammunition to protect your supply. Let's hope that you never have to use it, but given the potential for civil unrest, it's always better to be prepared. Besides, even if never used, my guess is that prices of both guns and ammunition will rise sharply, particularly if the government limits their future availability through legislation. Just think about it as another investment. I'm bullish on metal, and there is plenty of lead in bullets.

Get Good at Fixing Things

We live in an economy where if something breaks, it is usually less expensive to throw it away and buy a new one than it is to have it repaired or to try to repair it ourselves. (It's sometimes actually less expensive to buy a whole new computer printer than to replace an empty cartridge in the one you already have.) This situation came about in part because China has kept the value of the yuan against the dollar artificially low. As the dollar continues to drop, and China continues its policy of gradually loosening constraints on the yuan, artificially low prices will rise and U.S. residents will be forced to economize.

That means it will no longer make sense to toss that radio that's stopped working, or buy a new dress for every social occasion. Knowing how to fix small appliances, sew clothes, grow vegetables, and engage in other lost domestic arts of our grandparents' generation will stand you in good stead in the coming decade. They lived comfortably with fewer purchases, and had the satisfaction of being much more self-sufficient than we are today. Learning how to do the same will not only save you a bundle on discarded products that are no longer inexpensive to replace, but you'll find yourself with marketable skills. Neighbors who need their clothes mended or the fuse replaced in their electric appliances will happily pay you in cash or in barter for your trouble. That will provide extra money to add to your savings—or cover growing expenses as prices continue their climb.

The next 10 years will be difficult, but the coming economic adjustments will bring some real benefits. With U.S. consumers spending less, our trade imbalance will improve. I hope our government will respond to the crisis by finally instituting the kinds of measures and controls needed to make the dollar a safe and strong currency once again. And absurdly high prices for big-ticket items made possible by easy credit may return to reality in an environment where having a pulse is no longer enough to qualify for a loan.

This means real estate will become more affordable. As real estate prices collapse, the prospect of meaningful home ownership will again be within the reach of average U.S. residents. Provided they have the discipline and the wherewithal to actually save a 20 percent down payment, they will be able to buy a house without simultaneously mortgaging their futures. Despite higher interest rates, bigger down payments and lower balances will mean housing will take a smaller chunk out of the typical homeowner's paycheck. And with much lower real estate prices and higher interest rates on savings, the 20 percent down payment will be much easier to save!

The rate of ever-increasing college tuitions, which are currently inflated to unrealistic heights because widely available long-term student loans make it easier to go to college will also slow down, though students will wind up spending much of their working lives paying back those loans. Thirty or 40 years ago, young people could attend college without taking out a loan, as my father did, by working a part-time job and saving up from a summer job. Today, without rich parents or full scholarships, graduating from college debt-free is close to impossible.

In the short run, the coming credit crunch will mean fewer people attending college—an unnecessary expense in many professions—and heading straight into the workforce instead. But as loans dry up and enrollments decline, colleges will be forced to find ways to economize, and bring tuitions back to affordable levels. That will mean a new generation of college graduates will be able to start their careers without already facing decades of debt.

Parting Words

My aim in this chapter, and throughout this book, has been to prepare you to be in the best position possible to weather the coming economic storm with as little disruption as possible. To do this will require a return to the ethic of our parents' generation, when the norm was to save up for the things we wanted to buy, rather than simply charging whatever we couldn't afford to credit card debt that might never be fully repaid.

Cutting out credit card spending won't be a matter of choice for most U.S. citizens. I believe foreign creditors will dramatically reduce their investment in U.S. markets within the next year or two. That will derail the easy-credit gravy train that's gotten so many people so deep into credit card debt. If you're among them, getting those balances down as quickly as possible should be your number-one priority.

Your next biggest priority should be to start saving, bucking the dispiriting trend toward negative savings for U.S. residents overall in the past few years. U.S. residents who are counting on their home or stock market portfolios to provide a nest egg will be badly disappointed in the next decade—in fact, I predict these supposedly rock-solid investments will lose value instead of appreciating.

Cutting expenses where you can, learning to fix or make items rather than buy new ones, as well as buying large items secondhand rather than new, should help you build your savings more quickly. Whatever savings you create, it's vitally important to invest them as quickly as possible into non-dollar investments such as foreign stocks, commodities, and precious metals. Don't leave them in a U.S.-based savings account, money market, or mutual fund—or else your savings will lose value faster than you can sock them away.

Chapter Twelve

Pack Your Bags

~

*Emigrating Can Save
Wealth and Taxes*

THE UNITED STATES is no longer the land of opportunity it once was. For hundreds of years, ambitious, enterprising people wanted a better life and, despairing of finding it in Europe or Asia or Latin America, packed up their belongings and families and headed to the United States. In those days, low taxes and minimal regulation in our country provided a growing economy, coupled with social, political, and religious freedoms. That created a chance at wealth and a better lifestyle than they ever could have had at home.

The past two decades have seen a reversal of this long tradition. Entrepreneurial U.S. citizens may soon pack their bags and set off to the emerging markets of Eastern Europe, Asia, and Latin America to seek their fortunes in markets that are not overburdened with regulations or taxation.

These days, the trend toward emigrating from the United States for economic purposes has mainly been the province of the super wealthy looking to lower their tax liabilities, or of retirees, armed with Social Security payments in overvalued dollars that enable them to enjoy higher standards of living abroad than they can at home. This has been a particularly convenient option for those U.S. citizens who did not really save enough to retire comfortably here, so the choice was either to lie on the beach in an expatriate enclave in Costa Rica or to continue the rat race back home.

However, as the dollar continues its descent and eventually collapses, many of these expatriates will be forced to return home, as their dollars will no longer afford them the comforts that led them abroad in the first place. Unfortunately, the situation at home will not be much better, requiring most to go back to work.

How Can You Decide If You Will Need a Haven?

If things turn ugly, more and more people will find their lives in the United States becoming less and less livable. So emigrating abroad may offer an attractive alternative for many ordinary U.S. citizens, particularly the young and ambitious. Indeed, it may be the only viable option for people trapped in a highly taxed, heavily regulated, inflation-ravaged economy, where government policies prevent market forces from providing the opportunities available elsewhere.

When I wrote this chapter in the summer of 2008, the skies were certainly darkening with the clouds of economic collapse, but up till now U.S. residents have felt only the first few raindrops of the coming storm. So far, the government's response has amounted to an unhelpful continuation of its traditional economic policy: Borrow from abroad to prevent U.S. citizens from feeling the effects of a necessary economic adjustment. This was the logic behind the 2008 economic stimulus that put a check into every taxpayer's mailbox at the cost of even higher national debt, and the Federal Reserve's assistance in bailing out Bear Stearns when it tripped over its own subprime greed and was mortally wounded in the fall of 2007.

Written before the 2008 presidential election, I couldn't know for sure who the next U.S. president would be (although the smart money was clearly on Barack Obama), but by the time you read this book the outcome will have been decided. More important, I don't know for sure how the new government, whoever leads it, will respond to the crisis as it evolves, but if it sticks to the current script, it will keeping spending, printing, and borrowing from abroad to try to preserve a lifestyle that our country can no longer afford. This will only ensure that the crisis will be deeper and be more painful than it needs to be, requiring 10 or even 20 years before it is resolved. This will be especially true if President Obama follows though with his pledge to raise taxes on the very people we will depend on to provide the savings, production, and jobs our economy will so badly need.

For the United States to regain its economic strength, we need to allow for capital formation and encourage entrepreneurship. We must stop discouraging savings though inflation, punishing work through taxation, stifling growth through regulation, and start providing an environment where business can be creative and flourish.

If this happens, even those U.S. citizens who've had the foresight and discipline to save may still find themselves struggling to remain solvent as inflation rises. Worse, they may see their hard-earned savings subjected to new and onerous taxes, or policies that forbid them from taking their funds overseas. If you see the government heading in this direction, your smartest move might be to get out while you still can.

There is another possibility, though. Faced with an economic crisis they can no longer disguise, our national leaders might finally get it. With the economy completely unraveling and no longer able to borrow from abroad, the government may come to understand what it's been doing wrong for the past few decades. That realization could be the beginning of some real and badly needed reforms that will finally get the American economy headed in the right direction.

For the United States to regain its economic strength, we need to allow for capital formation and encourage entrepreneurship. We must stop discouraging savings though inflation, punishing work through taxation, stifling growth through regulation, and start providing an environment where business can be creative and flourish. That requires wholesale elimination of burdensome regulation; dramatically lowering taxes, especially on savings and investment; and substantially decreasing the size of government in general. Ideally, this would included dismantling entire departments (such as Education, Transportation, Housing, Energy,

Commerce, Homeland Security, and Agriculture); closing agencies such as the Securities and Exchange Commission (SEC) and Food and Drug Administration (FDA); firing other useless government employees such as statisticians and economists; eliminating many misguided social programs and means testing; and eventually abolishing all entitlements, especially Social Security. In so doing, we would then be able to abolish the taxes—personal and corporate income taxes and FICA taxes—needed to fund these endeavors.

Reforms like these, even if not as dramatic as I would like, would allow a balanced, dynamic, healthy, and prosperous economy to reemerge. We would see growing employment and plentiful opportunities to create wealth here at home. To be frank, even with the best of all possible reforms, I don't believe economic opportunities here will equal those in other countries, at least for the next several years. But if meaningful free-market reforms are really put in place, the next greatest emerging market could well be the United States.

It's hard to know which way the political winds will blow, though it seems a real long shot that unemployed voters struggling to make mortgage payments on homes with negative equity, while dealing with the high costs of food, energy, and other basic necessities, would vote for four more years of it—and that's what a vote for John

McCain might be perceived to be. In any case, the best strategy is to be prepared for anything—to have the flexibility to move someplace else if it becomes necessary, though you may hope it won't. So, whether you're drawn to the idea of living in an exotic locale, or whether you love the United States and want to stay forever, now is the time to plan for the possibility of living an expatriate life.

Where Should You Go?

Your choice of destination will depend partly on where you are in your working life and what your plans are for your future. If you're retired or nearing retirement age, then choosing a new home based on lifestyle considerations, such as climate, cost of living, and the availability of high quality and affordable health care, are likely to be your primary considerations.

However, if you're planning to retire and live off your investments, there's one thing you *must* keep in mind: It is likely that the only way to do this will be with non-U.S. dollar investments that produce non-U.S. dollar income streams.

By contrast, if you're midcareer or early in your career, you probably hope to continue building wealth so as to guarantee a comfortable future for yourself and your family. If that's the case, consider moving—as immigrants coming to the United States once did—to a place where economic activity is on the rise, and where opportunities for building wealth will be all around you.

Right now, the most rapid growth in the world can be found in the BRIC countries: Brazil, Russia, India, and China, and my personal preference would be China. Economic growth in each of these nations has outstripped that in the United States by a wide margin.

As an illustration, an index of all shares listed on the New York Stock Exchange rose 6.58 percent during 2007. That same year, the Russian stock market grew 11.54 percent, the Bovespa index of most-traded Sao Paulo stocks rose 44 percent, India's Sensex index of benchmark stocks was up 47.1 percent, and the Shanghai Composite Index rose 96.7 percent.

Right now, the most rapid growth in the world can be found in the BRIC countries: Brazil, Russia, India, and China, and my personal preference would be China.

It's not hard to see why the BRICs are where all the excitement is: As the United States gave up its leadership as a manufacturing nation, these countries stepped into the breach so that now most manufactured consumer goods purchased in the United States were made in one of the BRICs or its neighbors. Not only that, but service workers from BRIC nations now answer help-desk calls, read X-rays, write software, and prepare tax returns. Ironically, despite America's ballyhooed transition to a service economy, we still import billions of dollars in services, as well as manufactured goods, from the BRICs.

And while much of the attention may be focused on Brazil, Russia, India, and China, it's important to note that each represents an entire region rife with opportunity. Not only Brazil, but much of Latin America is fertile ground for building wealth. The same is true of Eastern Europe and Southeast Asia.

There's also a secondary effect of all the BRIC activity. These rapidly developing manufacturing nations have created vastly increased demand for raw materials, such as minerals and oil, and also foodstuffs and other goods as local living standards improve. That's led to economic growth in nations such as Canada, Australia, and New Zealand, which provide raw materials, energy, and food. This increased demand has spurred economic growth in these countries, which also have sounder governmental policies than those in the United States. So these should also be good places to build wealth for years to come with the added benefit of not having to master another language.

What will you do once you get there? If you're not planning to live off your investments or retirement income, then you have two choices: Get a job, or go into business for yourself. In Chapter 10, I provided lots of guidance as to which industries and professions have the greatest potential for a solid future in the United States. While I stand by those predictions, depending on what our government does, it may still pay to pursue those vocations abroad, where a stronger currency and more vibrant economy might mean you can do even better than at home. And if you are determined to earn a living in one of the areas that I identified as soon to be in decline, seeking opportunities abroad may be your most viable option.

The best way to build wealth in the BRICs is to start a business of your own.

The best way to build wealth in the BRICs is to start a business of your own. So if you've ever had any inclination toward the entrepreneurial life, I urge you to consider giving it a try if you move to one of these economies. By far, the biggest barrier to entry for new business is government regulation and taxation. So you greatly increase your chances of success if you minimize these factors. In addition, having a potential customer base that is growing in affluence and not already saddled with debt is a huge plus. Both of these dynamics exist abroad, and to find them I say, "Go east, young man."

Of course there is plenty of opportunity in the developed world as well. Singapore, Hong Kong (though officially a part of China), Switzerland, and Ireland are all good choices. These nations have lower taxes and fewer regulations than most, and thus provided fertile ground for both entrepreneurship and employment. I also like the Scandinavian countries. While they are historically known for having heavily socialized economies, the pendulum is now clearly swinging in the other direction. Also, many Eurozone economies will benefit from the strength of their currency and Europe's increased importance in the global pecking order. If you are more adventurous, you might consider the nations of the Persian Gulf, such as Dubai, Qatar, Kuwait, or the United Arab Emirates. Flush with petro dollars and unburdened by taxes or regulation, the Arab world seems destined to reclaim a more prominent role in the years ahead.

Other Factors to Consider

As the U.S. economy tanks, you're likely to fare better almost anywhere else. That gives you a large number of countries to choose from. The BRICs and their neighbors may offer the most vibrant economies, but what country makes most sense for you, personally? Following are some factors to weigh.

Immigration Laws

Moving permanently to a new country, especially if you're bringing your savings with you, is a complex endeavor that will probably require professional legal assistance. Immigration laws vary from country to country and may also depend on your background and your economic and family circumstances. As a vast generalization, emerging economies such as the BRICs are typically easier to get into than mature ones, because there is more need for new workers and more room in the market for new entrepreneurs. In any case, look into immigration laws very carefully when making your choice.

Banking Environment

This may not determine your choice of a new home, but it is an important issue you will have to consider carefully once you choose your destination. Setting up an account is very easy in many countries, more difficult in others. You will need not only to review local banking regulations but, if you can, find out from expatriate the U.S. citizens who've done it or other trusted sources what banking in your new country will actually be like.

As a twenty-first-century emigrant you have one huge advantage: Internet banking makes it easier, more convenient, and more affordable to live in one country and bank in another than it has ever been before. That means you can, if you choose, set up a bank account in your new country well in advance of emigrating there, so that you can begin transferring funds in cash that will be converted into the local currency and thus protected against the dollar's continuing decline. (As described earlier, this may be something you choose to do in any case, even if you're not planning to emigrate.)

Just as important, it also means that you are not obligated to keep your money in the country where you choose to live. For instance, some U.S. citizens who move to Mexico set up bank accounts in nearby Belize because such accounts provide greater privacy and asset protection than a local account would. Likewise, many people doing business or working throughout Asia choose to do their banking in Hong Kong, thanks to its very nonintrusive policies. So if the banking environment in the country where you plan to live is not to your liking, think outside the borders, and make sure to investigate nearby alternatives.

Two final points, which should probably go without saying: (1) If you're a United States citizen, you must report any income earned outside the United States when you file your U.S. tax return. It's a crime not to, and not worth the trouble you will get into if you are caught. (2) Only do your banking with a solid bank with a long history and sterling reputation, even if a brand-new, no-name bank offers a better deal. This is especially important if you're banking in a country that lacks government guarantees for bank accounts (such as the Federal Deposit Insurance Corporation, or FDIC, provides in the United States).

Language

This will obviously be the biggest limiting factor for most U.S. citizens, since the majority of us do not succeed in learning a second language, or at least not very well, during a typical U.S. education. If you would be comfortable living only somewhere where English is spoken, your best choices may be Canada, Australia, and New Zealand. It's also worth noting that, while there are more than 20 different languages throughout India, English is widely spoken there, although it's a very different version of English than we're accustomed to at home.

If you already speak a foreign language, that may help dictate your choice as to where to move. If you don't speak a foreign language but are willing to learn a new one, I recommend Mandarin Chinese. Though it can be a challenge for Westerners, the effort of learning Mandarin Chinese may literally pay off because China offers unparalleled economic opportunities.

Lifestyle

If you're retiring or planning to retire, then lifestyle issues will be your primary concern in choosing a new home. Some expatriates like the idea of living in a warm climate, and if that's your goal, there are plenty of warm-climate countries on our list that also offer economic opportunity.

Beyond climate, you should consider other lifestyle factors that are important to you. If you like the idea of having servants provide for your every need, then Southeast Asia may be an attractive choice. If you like the idea of living in a neighborhood where you can leave your door unlocked, consider Canada, New Zealand, or Australia. If you like your U.S. lifestyle, then living in Canada is probably more similar to living in the United States than any other country, although retirees in Mexico report that its malls have many of the same chain stores that you would find in a mall at home.

If getting the best possible education for your children is a major concern, Canada might seem the most obvious choice. However, many foreign countries have international schools where instruction is in English and where many of the teachers are from the United States and are well experienced at helping students prepare for competitive college admissions.

Personal History

Your and your family's individual history may well be a primary factor in your choice of a new home. The United States has always been a nation of immigrants, and for many citizens whose parents, grandparents, or great-grandparents came from elsewhere, it might be logical to consider returning to those roots. For one thing, you may still have relatives in your family's country of origin. They may be delighted to meet their cousins from the United States, and happy to help you settle into your new home.

Your family history may also help you resolve immigration issues more easily. Some nations have policies granting special consideration to the children and even grandchildren of emigrated citizens; or your local family, if you still have one, may be able to help sponsor you for residency.

If You Stay Home

You'll be safest with an emigration plan in place in case the time comes when it's best to leave. Having said that, I recognize that some readers simply cannot leave the United States, because of family connections, age, or an attachment to their home country. If this is you, I recommend that you at least consider the possibility of moving within the United States, depending on where you're currently living.

───────────────── ∾ ─────────────────

If you live in a large urban area, especially one with an inner-city population, you may find that a bad place to be as the U.S. economy unravels.

─────────────────────────────────────

If you live in a large urban area, especially one with an inner-city population, you may find that a bad place to be as the U.S. economy unravels. Inflation will drive prices of food and other basics to unaffordable levels, and price controls may lead to outright shortages. Meanwhile, public assistance checks will either diminish as our spendthrift government finally runs out of money, or lose practically all their value because of massive inflation because our elected officials lack the political will to actually make the necessary cuts. On top of that, misguided government policies may lead to a sagging economy that will offer fewer job prospects than ever. It's a volatile combination that could prove dangerous for anyone living in or near a poor urban neighborhood.

At the same time, you may find that relocating to the suburbs gives you a plentiful supply of very affordable housing. As long commutes, expensive gas, and over-extended borrowers at first make these properties less desirable than those more centrally located, a sea of foreclosures will make for good bargains. Resist the temptation to buy too soon, and look for available rentals until prices have completely collapsed.

It's hard to predict how the government will react and what other U.S. residents will do as our economy crashes, but there is a wide range of possibilities that could include the rationing of electricity (already seen in California during the Enron days) and even fighting over food. So you'd be better off in a suburban or even rural area, far from any urban center. The more self-sufficient you're able to be—for instance, growing your own vegetables, using your own well water, and providing solar power for at least some of the electricity in your home—the better off you will be in case things go really wrong.

Parting Words

The lesson of this chapter is not that you have to leave the United States. Indeed, I deeply hope that our misguided federal government will recognize its folly and take corrective action before our economy disintegrates completely. If this happens, then the United States will continue to be a great place to live for many people, although many of us will have to tone down the profligate lifestyles we're accustomed to. This is why I personally have no plans to leave the country for now (though in the figurative sense my money left years ago) and I hope to be an active participant and investor in the rebuilding process.

If, however, our government continues its destructive policies of unbridled spending and—because it can no longer borrow from abroad—resorts to raising taxes and printing more money to make up the difference, then living in the United States may become very difficult indeed. Those of us who have wisely saved our money and now have substantial investments may find those investments heavily taxed, inflated away, or even outright confiscated by a government desperate for funds. In this scenario, your best bet will be to get out. In fact, in June 2008, when this chapter was written, a bill was signed into law making it far more expensive to settle permanently in another country by requiring any unrealized capital gains on worldwide assets to be taxed as if all assets had been sold the day prior to expatriation.

The good news is that there is a long list of countries with stronger economies than ours, so you have many choices of places to go. In some, such as Canada, New Zealand, and Australia, you'll arrive already speaking the language. In others,

(continued)

you may need to learn a foreign language first, but the economic rewards you'll gain should make the extra study well worth the effort. And even if you arrive less than fully fluent, since English is the most widely spoken second language in the world, your transition would probably not be too difficult.

If things turn ugly, you'll need to pull your affairs and family together, and depart for your new home as quickly as you can. That means now is the time to prepare, with research about immigration laws and banking, comparing climates and lifestyles in various countries, and creating a definite plan as to where and how you will emigrate. With airfares lower than they're likely to be in the future, now is a good time to visit other countries, connect with U.S. citizens already living there (or your long-lost relatives), and see what life is like on the ground.

You may be pleasantly surprised to learn that foreign lifestyles and the overall benefits of emigrating are more attractive than you expected. You may decide to plan your departure right now. Or you may simply decide to keep your plan at the ready, in case conditions here go from bad to worse.

Let's hope you will never be forced to use it.

Chapter Thirteen

The Light at the End
of the Tunnel

—◈—

How to Make It Shine on You

THE MUSICAL NUMBER whose title I purloined for my opening chapter, "Let's Do the Time Warp Again," has a lyric that goes, in part, "Madness takes its toll." How aptly those words set the tone for this closing chapter.

Astonishingly, amid $140-a-barrel oil, a collapsing auto sector, soaring food prices, massive foreclosures, empty restaurant tables, failing retailers, and insolvent banks, our government, as I write this in June 2008, assures us we are not in a recession and our economy is fundamentally strong, its resilience demonstrated yet again by GDP growth accompanied by low inflation and low unemployment. Having read the preceding chapters, you know you have to take government economic information with a grain of salt. But I still find it fascinating that in the face of such dramatic evidence to the contrary, the government persists in using selected technicalities and creative statistics to assure us all is well.

Government statistics are blatantly and deliberately manipulated, not because some sinister conspiracy perceived uniquely by Peter Schiff is afoot, as some TV hosts are fond of alleging, but because they have to be if the Federal Reserve wants us to believe it can simultaneously fight inflation and pursue a stimulative monetary policy, a contradiction in terms. Chairman Bernanke calls it his "dual mandate," but that sounds to me like gobbledygook. With an unbalanced economy, and under political pressure to both print money and combat inflation, the government can't possibly give us meaningful numbers.

What really gets me, though, is that the economic realities being hidden behind these misleading government statistics are potentially catastrophic and urgently require action. Our economy today is about as solid as a subprime mortgage or a late-1990s Internet stock, but the crowd in charge didn't see a problem then and I doubt they see one now. These are the same people who thought things were just great in 2005, 2006, and 2007. They didn't understand then that we were living in a bubble economy, and now that the bubble has burst, they don't understand why we need anything more than a quick jump-start to get things back on track.

To restore viability to our economy, we need to start saving again so we can become producers again. The consumer-based economy will contract along with all its malls and other trappings, However, to get from where we are to where we need to be, a recession has to be allowed to run its course, however difficult that course proves to be. But therein lies the crux of our problem: It runs against conventional political wisdom to allow voters to swallow bad-tasting medicine, even when it is the only way to cure the disease. That has to change.

What happens after the elections in November 2008 will be a key determinant of the economy's future. Post-election programs designed to encourage more spending both by the government and by individuals will lead ruinously in the wrong direction. But there is another fork in the road, no less painful to travel, but leading eventually to renewed prosperity. More on the election in a minute.

The Box the Federal Reserve Is In

The Fed's dilemma is that its two options for getting the American economy on a viable long-term course require at least eight years or so of a substantially lower standard of living for most people. There's no quick and easy way to do it.

One of its options is to do nothing, meaning it keeps interest rates artificially low, which is causing inflation abroad to rise dramatically, particularly where currencies are pegged to the dollar. Central banks are thus raising rates to combat their own inflation and considering abandoning dollar pegs where they exist. Both actions will accelerate the dollar's decline. Trading partners, gradually realizing they could replace the American market with their own, may cut the American *Titanic* loose to sink on its own. With nobody supporting our currency, the dollar will drop like a stone. But to keep rates low and let inflation run out of control risks hyperinflation à la Weimar Germany, an economic death sentence.

The other option is to raise interest rates from 2 percent to 8 percent or so (or perhaps much higher), which would reduce inflation but trigger massive foreclosures and defaults in credit card and other consumer debt. This paper was securitized like subprime mortgage paper, and defaults will impact capital markets in a similar way. Higher corporate borrowing costs would lower corporate profits and stock prices. Raising interest rates high enough to eliminate inflation will precipitate a 1930s Great Depression scenario, this time with rising instead of falling consumer prices. Bernanke has to let the economy collapse today so it can be prosperous tomorrow and to salvage any fraction of the dollar's value. If he doesn't do it now, he'll have to raise rates higher a year from now to combat additional inflation created in the meantime. If he digs in his heels, determined to reflate the bubble at all cost, the dollar's value will be completely destroyed, an economic Armageddon that will unleash untold havoc.

Why We Should Take a Solutions Approach to the Crisis and Look at Some Things Differently

I don't think we're going to see any light at the end of the tunnel until we have a clear, objective understanding of how we got into this mess in the first place. There is a tendency whenever major problems occur in the economy to place blame on external factors and to assume that the external factors can be prevented from causing similar problems in the future by expanding the government's regulatory powers. The problem I have with this kind of thinking is that it makes government bigger and more intrusive without ever getting at the root of the problem, which is usually the government itself. The other thing it does is reduce the sphere in which market forces move freely and would otherwise prevent the problem from recurring. Finally, as we face the challenge of rebuilding an economy, whatever lesson might have been learned from the government's role in the problem is lost on us because it was never brought to light in the first place.

The real estate meltdown provides an excellent example. Here we are about to give the Federal Reserve Board new powers to regulate mortgage lenders, appraisers, and other parties to a crisis that would never have occurred if the Fed hadn't taken upon itself the responsibility, better left to the free market, of determining what interest rates should be, particularly true with the absurdly low rates set after the bursting of the tech bubble and the tragedy of September 11, 2001.

The Fed's decision to set rates at artificially low levels to stimulate activity and growth in the real estate sector was directly responsible for the environment that naturally spawned such innovations as teaser rates, negative amortization loans, and other variations on adjustable-rate mortgages, which in turn had consequences that were extremely problematic. But the mortgage brokers and lenders weren't responsible for the root cause of the crisis, nor were the investment banks that securitized the mortgages, nor the hedge funds and institutions that purchased them. The Federal Reserve was. Yet the Fed is now being rewarded with additional powers to regulate

Wall Street as well. So the fox ends up guarding the hen-house, which is bad enough, but anybody looking for the guiding lesson of the crisis probably wouldn't find it. The real lesson is this: Interest rates represent the price of money (or more precisely, the price of credit). A government agency has no more business deciding what the price of money should be than it has deciding the price of a pair of tennis shoes. Why are we so surprised that central government planning works no better when it comes to setting the price of money than it does in setting prices for other goods?

The price of oil is being blamed on speculators, big oil companies, environmentalists, and other external factors—but never on the Federal Reserve, which created the inflation that debased the dollars in which oil is traded and is thus principally responsible for increased oil prices. Priced in gold, which adjusts for inflation, oil has actually changed very little in price.

What worries me most, however, is the almost automatic backlash that attributes the present economic collapse to a failure of capitalism and free-market economics and turns it into an argument for expanded government. Never mind that government created a crisis that the free market would have avoided altogether; the problem with this case of mistaken identity is that it almost certainly will result in expanded government, much as the New Deal did during the Great Depression. Of course, the greater problem today is that we can barely afford the old New Deal, let alone the modern version we're about to be dealt!

The approach we need to take to our present crisis is not to expand government, but rather to understand government's role in creating the problem. The solution is to limit and control the power of government, not to create more unnecessary regulation to interfere with the free market forces that would have prevented the problem.

Thoughts on the Upcoming Presidential Election and How It Might Affect Our Economy

I think what we've learned from this historic economic breakdown is that it represents a colossal failure of government planning. When you have the government taking control of something as important as setting interest rates, this is the kind of disaster you get.

At this critical political juncture, are we going to compound the problem by giving the government even more power, making it even bigger, and putting it in a position to do even more damage? The alternative, of course, is letting the free market self-correct, which I believe in strongly but which is not, I'm afraid, the way Americans are inclined to lean in a time of economic crisis.

The impending failures of Freddie Mac and Fannie Mae, events I forecast in my book *Crash Proof,* in commentaries on my web site, and on television, and the government's intention to bail them out, is a huge step in the wrong direction. These quasi-governmental agencies, with their implied government guarantees, provided much of the air that inflated the housing bubble, and should be allowed to fail. Instead, they will be pumped up with more government money, compounding the fundamental problems in the housing market and worsening inflation.

In fact, early on in the housing crisis, most in government and on Wall Street were still so clueless that these agencies were actually touted as being the solution to the problem. In sharp contrast, I wrote in an August 2007 commentary entitled "It's a Shoo-In":

> In order to breathe life into the dying secondary market for nonconforming mortgages, some have suggested that Fannie Mae and Freddie Mac be allowed to buy jumbo mortgages. This overlooks the problem that many of these larger mortgages also feature adjustable rates that will likely show greater default levels when payments reset higher. Allowing Fannie and Freddie to buy larger loans now merely sets up a more expensive federal bailout down the road, as both of these entities themselves will likely need to be bailed out when the conforming ARMs they already insure go bad as well.

Bailing out Freddie and Fannie, as well as all schemes to bail out overextended homeowners and artificially prop up home prices are doomed to failure, and will only compound the problems they are attempting to solve. The recent failure of California-based IndyMac, a former leader in nontraditional mortgage lending, resulting in long lines of angry depositors, is but the tip of the iceberg. As more banks fail and the FDIC runs out of funds, the Fed's printing presses will be operating until they run out of ink.

Without getting into a contentious political discussion, I do see a parallel between the 1976 election of Jimmy Carter and the Reagan succession in 1980. Carter had taken office at a time when inflation and unemployment were issues. Voters were disenchanted by Gerald Ford and alienated by his pardon of Richard Nixon, whose abuses of power were still very much on their minds, and whose failed policies led to higher inflation and unemployment. The mood was very strong for a change from the traditional ways of Washington. The economy was so bad that Gerald Ford was even challenged in the primary by Ronald Reagan, who at the time was dismissed by the media and the party elites as too outside the mainstream to be electable. Carter ran as a Southern modernist and Washington outsider. He promised change and won. A similar situation exists today.

The Carter administration proved to be a turnoff and a disappointment for a majority of Americans, as the bad economy he inherited got even worse under his stewardship. As a result, the emergence of Ronald Reagan, an improbable candidate under normal circumstances, was actually welcomed as a timely alternative. Voters generally bought his mantra that government was the problem, not the solution, and he won the election. Reagan and Federal Reserve Chairman Paul Volcker took on double-digit inflation with double-digit interest rates, inflation was pronounced dead, striking air controllers were simply fired in a no-nonsense way, and the Reagan years generally got high marks. The mainstream world was now finally safe for a conservative promising limited government, provided his predecessor had exhausted the public's tolerance for big government. Unfortunately, Reagan never really followed through with his promise to rein in government spending, the consequences of which we are struggling with today.

Similar to Gerald Ford, John McCain had one challenger in particular whose message of limited government and sound money resonated with a small but organized minority. I am referring to Congressman Ron Paul, who, despite being marginalized by his other opponents and the mainstream media, struck a chord unheard elsewhere in modern politics, and managed to raise more money than any of the mainstream Republican alternatives.

The 2008 election features two candidates likely to make the current problems worse. Ironically, Barack Obama, whose policies would likely prove even more disastrous than McCain's, probably represents the lesser of the two evils. This is because Obama is perceived to be the candidate of big government, while McCain has wrapped himself in the false trappings of small government.

In the unlikely event McCain wins, he will be the Herbert Hoover of the modern era, completely discrediting capitalism in the minds of the electorate and setting the stage for a disastrous ideological counterreaction in the election that follows.

If Obama wins, however, while the economy will fare even worse, it will at least be clear that big government is to blame. By the end of Obama's term, the voters will have had such a bellyful of noxious government solutions that the mere thought of any more will put them squarely at the wheel of the porcelain bus. In such an environment, a Ron Paul type of Republican, dismissed as unelectable à la Ronald Reagan in 1976, may actually be in a position to capture the White House in 2012 and finish the job Ronald Reagan started.

Ultimately, we are going to need a free-market president, who understands sound money and Austrian economics and has the toughness, courage, and leadership talent to take the bull by the horns and begin the process of shrinking government, dismantling programs we can't afford, minimizing regulation and taxation so businesses can operate without competitive disadvantages, and generally taking the steps that will put us on a path to becoming a nation of savers and producers once again. If suffering though four years of hellishly misguided big government is the price we pay for true reform, it may in the end be worth it.

Tunnels and Lights

When can we expect to see that light at the end of the tunnel and be sure we're seeing daylight and not another train coming the other way? When will it be safe to start bringing our money home and an auspicious time to begin investing again in the United States?

The short answer is: Sit tight until 2012, when at least one new presidential term will be over. Here's the longer answer: Of importance overriding all else, the fundamental economic reform we've been talking about must be firmly in place and forward momentum be irrevocably underway.

The chances are it will take longer for these prerequisites to be in place, and when they are, don't expect a public mood of confidence and optimism. To the contrary, the most auspicious time to invest, to use the words of the late, great Sir John Templeton, will be at the point of maximum pessimism. That's when stock valuations, as measured by high yields, low price-earnings ratios, and market prices that are low relative to book value (or below it), will represent the best buying opportunities, again assuming economic reform has begun.

Why Lower Living Standards Will Hurt More This Time

The declining dollar's reduced purchasing power means commensurate declines in our standard of living. But off-setting adjustments that were possible in the 1970s are not available this time around. One dynamic claimed by many to be missing in today's inflation is the wage-price spiral. Often cited as having contributed to inflation, both prices and wages (the price of labor) actually rose as the result of inflation. The dreaded wage-price spiral was merely the government's way of confusing the public with regard to the true cause of inflation. Today, however, the fact that wages are rising more slowly than other prices is somehow being hailed as good news. Prices are rising, but we're told not to worry, since wages are not. What a relief! Stagnant domestic wages in the face of escalating goods prices only serve to make today's inflation that much more painful. Nor is it consoling that wages abroad, in contrast, are rising to keep pace with the inflation we're exporting and then are being passed on in the prices of stuff we're importing.

But that's only half of it. In the 1970s when the dollar lost 70 percent of its value and things got tight at home, women started going to work. It has since been spun as women's liberation, and in a sense it was, but economic necessity forced it, and in today's typical household husband and wife both need jobs to make ends meet.

So what do we do this time around? Send the kids to work? We reduce consumption, plain and simple!

Demand destruction, a concept I referred to earlier, is often brought up in business discussions on TV as a force that could bring high oil prices down. The problem with that argument is that since the United States doesn't exist in a vacuum, demand destroyed here by reduced purchasing power is re-created in other markets where purchasing power is increasing. The result is that Americans will consume less, but pay more for what they do consume.

By no means confined to oil, demand destruction in the United States will cut consumption across the board. But where a product or commodity is in demand globally, the economic effect will be offset by increased consumption elsewhere, and price pressure will remain strong. In the automobile industry, for example, sales are collapsing here just as they are surging in Russia, which has recently overtaken Germany as Europe's largest automobile market. So the steel once used to make cars for us is now being used to make cars for the Russians. As Americans are priced out of markets, others are priced in. Consumption declines here, yet prices continue to rise because global demand increases.

The Positive Side of Demand Destruction

Demand destruction, however unpleasant its effects on human comfort, in economic terms reduces consumption and restores equilibrium. Once an economy, however downsized or otherwise constructively reformed, is thus restored to health, economic growth becomes feasible and investment opportunity follows.

For example, the domestic airline industry will eventually adjust to demand destruction caused by the inability of enough Americans to pay ticket prices that would enable airlines to operate profitably. How they'll do it is above my pay grade, but if a domestic airline industry survives, it will have found a way to make itself viable. At some point in the process, it follows that airline shares, most likely following bankruptcy reorganizations, will be an attractive investment.

Or take the oil industry. The United States, with its present capacity, produces some 10 percent of the world's output but accounts for 25 percent of the world's consumption. I predict the day will come when the United States is a net exporter of oil, regardless of what happens with offshore drilling and alternative energy sources, because of demand destruction. We'll consume less oil until we bring our consumption into line with our ability to buy it. This is another investment opportunity.

Similar positive adjustments will occur in college tuitions, health care costs, and multitudinous other areas where the government got in the way of the free market and through the extension of easy credit caused prices to become too high. As the credit dries up, so will the high prices it enabled. Universities will have to streamline their costs and offer an education product that students and their families can actually afford. Similarly, hospitals and doctors will need to become more efficient as well so patients can actually afford their services. Even the collapse in home prices is a blessing, as homes will be much more affordable and Americans will no longer have to take on so much debt to buy them.

But the bottom line is: Stay out of the dollar until the coast is clear. Personally, I'm optimistic, and if we wait long enough, our patience will be rewarded.